"Penned in an appealing, conversational style, Kiasunomics© *provides deep insights into how we can make better decisions in a complex world, if we knew what research has found. It provokes readers to reflect and pose questions of their own. I'm delighted that research at National University of Singapore has created practical impact for the nation and beyond."*

Professor Tan Eng Chye
Deputy President (Academic Affairs) and Provost, National University of Singapore

"I marvel at how the NUS professors can weave their research findings into a storybook. It's enlightening to see how much Economics can affect us. People will find this book interesting to read and benefit from their research."

Dr William Fung
Group Managing Director, Li & Fung Group

"Everyone interested in the value of big data can benefit from this book. The authors have been able to marry deep data analytics with empirical observations to come up with extremely interesting insights. In addition, the storytelling nature of the narrative makes it easy to follow and relate to. For non-Singaporeans, this is a ready primer of many behaviours that drive our country!"

Mr Piyush Gupta
Chief Executive Officer and Director, DBS Group

"This book is a delight to read. Interestingly, it coincides with the 2017 Nobel Prize in Economic Sciences awarded to one of the founding fathers of behavioural economics — an area of Economics adopted in this book. Kiasunomics© *resonates with the broader impact of Singaporean behavioural traits,* kiasuism *being one. The authors cleverly tell a number of stories, drawing on the findings of their rigorous academic work, to illustrate the economic consequences of seemingly innocuous or irrational decisions made by individuals. They have chosen a narrative style which allows serious academic literature to appeal to a broader readership."*

Dr Seek Ngee Huat

Chairman, Institute of Real Estate Studies and Practice Professor, National University of Singapore; Chairman, Global Logistic Properties Ltd

"Economics affects our daily lives profoundly. Yet, so few of us are aware of this. This book is a great gift to Singaporeans as it cleverly integrates research with storytelling to show the impact of Economics on our lives. I highly commend this very readable book to Singaporeans and others. You will have fun as you learn."

Professor Kishore Mahbubani

Dean, Lee Kuan Yew School of Public Policy, National University of Singapore, and co-author of *The ASEAN Miracle: A Catalyst for Peace*

Kiasunomics©

Stories of Singaporean Economic Behaviours

Kiasunomics©

Stories of Singaporean Economic Behaviours

Sumit Agarwal
Ang Swee Hoon
Sing Tien Foo

National University of Singapore

World Scientific

NEW JERSEY • LONDON • SINGAPORE • BEIJING • SHANGHAI • HONG KONG • TAIPEI • CHENNAI • TOKYO

Published by

World Scientific Publishing Co. Pte. Ltd.
5 Toh Tuck Link, Singapore 596224
USA office: 27 Warren Street, Suite 401-402, Hackensack, NJ 07601
UK office: 57 Shelton Street, Covent Garden, London WC2H 9HE

National Library Board, Singapore Cataloguing-in-Publication Data
Name(s): Agarwal, Sumit.
Title: Kiasunomics© : stories of Singaporean economic behaviours / Sumit Agarwal, Ang Swee Hoon, Sing Tien Foo.
Description: Singapore : World Scientific Publishing Co. Pte. Ltd., [2017]
Identifier(s): OCN 1005840043 | ISBN 978-981-3234-53-6 (paperback) | 978-981-3233-36-2 (hardcover)
Subject(s): LCSH: Economics—Psychological aspects. | Consumer behavior—Singapore.
Classification: DDC 330.019—dc23

British Library Cataloguing-in-Publication Data
A catalogue record for this book is available from the British Library.

For any available supplementary material, please visit
http://www.worldscientific.com/worldscibooks/10.1142/10799#t=suppl

Desk Editor: Jiang Yulin

Contents

Acknowledgements

Our thanks to our research collaborators as well as our National University of Singapore colleagues whose interesting and meaningful research help to make this book possible:

CHENG Shih Fen

CHOI Hyun Soo

CHOMSISENGPHET Souphala

CHONG Juin Kuan

DIAO Mi

GOETTE Lorenz

HE Jie

HO Teck Hua

HYUN Soo Choi

KEPPO Jussi

KOO Kang Mo

LIM Cheryl

LIU Haoming

PAN Jessica

PNG Ivan P.L.

QIAN Wenlan

QIN Yu

REEB David M

RENGARAJAN Satyanarain

TAN Poh Lin

TIEFENBECK Verena

VOLLMER Derek

WANG Davin Hong Yip
WONG Wei-Kang
YANG Yang
YI Fan
ZHANG Jian

Our heartfelt appreciation also extends to the organisations who generously shared their data with us so that research can be conducted to benefit the society.

The talented staff at World Scientific — Chua Hong Koon, Jiang Yulin and Amanda Yun — deserve praise for their role in shaping this book.

We also thank Professor Bernard Yeung and Ms Joan Tay at National University of Singapore Business School for their encouragement and support.

Finally, our overriding debt continues to be to our families who provided the time, support and inspiration to our research and preparation of this book.

Note from the Authors

Unless otherwise stated, values prefixed with simple dollar '$' are in Singapore dollar.

List of Acronyms

ATM	Automatic Teller Machine
BCA	Building and Construction Authority
CBD	Central Business District
CHAS	Community Health Assist Scheme
CL	Circle Line
COV	Cash over Valuation
CPF	Central Provident Fund
EMA	Energy Market Authority
ERP	Electronic Road Pricing
GDP	Growth Dividend Programme
GPS	Global Positioning System
GSS	Great Singapore Sale
GST	Goods and Services Tax
HDB	Housing & Development Board
IU	In-vehicle Unit
JB	Johor Bahru
KTM	Keretapi Tanah Melayu
LTA	Land Transport Authority
MOE	Ministry of Education
MRT	Mass Rapid Transit
NEA	National Environment Agency

NUS	National University of Singapore
Ph.D.	Doctor of Philosophy
PSI	Pollutant Standards Index
PUB	Public Utilities Board
SEC	Singapore Environment Council
UHI	Urban Heat Island

Glossary of Singlish Terms

Publisher's Note: The spelling of the Singlish terms found in this book may differ from its original/commonly known form. The varied spelling forms are based on the authors' understanding as well as the context of the storyline in which these terms are used.

Agak agak: Approximate/Guess

Ah/Hor/Lah/Leh/Lor/Mah/Meh: Singlish end-particles that function as many word-types – adverbs, modifiers, exclamations, etc. – depending on context. Often indicative of the speaker's feelings, emotions or tone at the moment of speech.

Ah Kong: Grandfather

Ah Mah: Grandmother

Aiyah/Aiyoh: An exclamation used to convey impatience or dismay

Alamak: Oh gosh

Ang moh: Western

Atas: Proud

Blanjah: Treat

Cheem: Difficult

Choon: Accurate/Timely

Chope: Reserve

Chumpo: Mixed

Dit dit: Straight

Eh/Hah: An interjection used to convey enquiry, surprise, or to elicit agreement

Fatt: Prosper

Gahmen: Government

Gao she: Teach from books

Gao yang: Teach to win

Go fly kite: Get lost

Gotong royong: Looking out for each other

Habis: Unfortunate finishing

Heng: Thank goodness

Hong bao: Red packet

Jiak kan tan: Eat potatoes, implying speaking in proper English like people who eat potatoes – Westerners

Kam sia: Thank you

Kena: Have

Kena ketuk: Got scammed

Ketuk: Cheated

Kiabor: Scared of wife

Kiasee: Scared to die

Kiasu: Scared to lose

Langah: Collision

Lei mo tuin tuin fatt tat: You prosper without having to do anything

Makan: Eat

Manjang: Irritable

Mata: Policeman

Pai kia: Naughty child

Pasar: Wet market

Qiong: Clash/Do quickly without thinking

Say: Death

Sayang: Wasteful

Sekali: Used for emphasis to demonstrate the contradictory behavior that may occur

Siao: Crazy

Sway: Cursed

Tahan: Tolerate

Tai tai: Wealthy woman

Ulu: Remote

Wah piang eh: Holy moly

Yah: An expression used to convey agreement

Introduction

Ask any person on the street: What comes to mind when thinking of 'Singapore'? The question is likely to induce responses like *cleanliness, low crime, a cultural melting pot, a street food haven, chewing gum ban* (which is not entirely true), and not forgetting *a* 'fine' *city*!

Our knowledge of this little island city is generally limited, consisting mostly of quaint anecdotes – one-off observations with little awareness – rather than a full understanding of the economics underlying Singaporeans' behaviours and decisions in their everyday lives.

But one thing we do know for sure is that Singaporeans are a competitive bunch. They have an intense fear of losing out or to put it in their unique local lingo, Singlish, they are *kiasu*.

Singaporeans do their best to stretch every dollar, to the extent of doing their grocery runs in Johor Bahru to take advantage of the weaker currency there. Petrol is cheaper across the Causeway too, thus giving them more bang for their buck. Enduring the long drive and snaking customs queue, they often ply the Singapore–Malaysia Causeway on weekends. They also pay top dollar to buy or rent homes near choice schools to give their pre-schoolers the best chance of gaining a place in these schools – to give them a head start in the highly competitive Singaporean education system.

It is also interesting to note that some Singaporeans do their family planning with the Chinese lunar calendar in mind – timing births to fall within the auspicious year of the Dragon owing to the belief that Dragon babies are as mighty and blessed as the mystical creature, which may then give them an edge in life.

Indian-born American-bred, Sumit was intrigued and fascinated by *kiasuism* and the Singaporean culture when he first arrived to become faculty at the National University of Singapore (NUS) Business School. Why were Singaporeans fixated with the number '8'? Why could he never find a taxi when he needed one? Piqued, he was certain of research opportunities behind these phenomena.

It is also his personal belief that since he works in Singapore for Singapore, his research must create impact for the nation and its people. After all, the research environment at NUS Business School encourages rigourous and relevant research that fulfills meaningful curiosity.

An unlikely partner-in-crime came in the form of Tien Foo, a professor at the Department of Real Estate in NUS. They began working together on research in finance, economics and real estate using logit models, binominal indicators, dummy variables and other econometric methods (say what?) to explain the world.

While seemingly uninteresting and incomprehensible, their research is among the few that looked into issues unique to Singapore, and offers a perspective that is not only relevant to Singaporeans but also to the rest of the world who may want to learn from this country.

Swee Hoon is a Marketing professor who was so captivated by Sumit's and Tien Foo's Singapore-based research that she decided to join them and use her marketing chops to transform their mumbo-jumbo academic work into pieces that most people can understand and enjoy.

The trio became good friends. One day, compelled to do more than just writing and publishing academic papers, Sumit suggested that they share what they have learnt from their research with a wider audience. The three friends agreed to write a book which will be read by more than just the few with Ph.D.s, bear insights to benefit the society, and embody the NUS Business School's core value of caring for the community through knowledge sharing.

And so, this book – *Kiasunomics©* – was born. This is our first attempt at storytelling; where we leave our comfort zone of formal, terse and often peculiar nomenclature (the formal names or terms for various things) academics are accustomed to, and bravely and humbly use our conversational voice and Singlish.

In our book, we explore everyday economic issues faced by Singaporeans through the life journey of Teng – from birth to adulthood – and examine how personal decisions have economic ramifications on daily living.

Each chapter is a standalone story and is intentionally not filled with references to theoretical economic arguments and models, research jargon, data analyses, or a series of tables to present the findings. Instead, each is crafted with a short easy-to-read tale that reflects the underlying economic intuition based on our research analyses of micro data using advanced econometric techniques.

To put simply, the idea behind this book is to use relevant and understandable research to demonstrate how seemingly innocuous decisions or events have economic bearing.

We begin with the decision by Teng's parents to have him as a Dragon baby and show how this decision affects his education, career and spending in the long haul. We will reveal why Dragon babies are not as fortunate as astrologers have us believe. The grown-up Teng in later chapters is a taxi driver from whom we learn how daily budgeting of finances can be poor financial planning.

The story follows with Teng's purchase of a flat based on superstitious beliefs and proximity to a choice school and a Mass Rapid Transit station. Do you know that contrary to common belief, there are more properties transacted during the Hungry Ghost month than the 8th lunar month? And that not all properties within the two-kilometre zone of a choice primary school enjoy similar premiums?

How do we know all these? Well, one early morning, while comfortably sipping tea on the balcony, Sumit noticed this very long line of cars across the road. Parents were dropping off their kids at the school there. Curious, he soon learned the measures *kiasu* parents would go to enrol their little ones in a choice school. But the decisions and actions of these parents had inadvertently caused a massive jam in the neighbourhood. "Hah!" thought Sumit, experiencing a Eureka moment, "That's a potential research question."

What about houses ending with the number '8'? Do they command a higher value because it brings good luck? Think again. In the story on Teng's hunt for a flat, we show that there's more to a lucky number than meets the eye.

In Chapter 7 of this story, Teng witnesses a childhood friend's brush with bankruptcy, which gives him a glimpse of the predicament faced by a number of Singaporeans prone to this plight. Call it profiling if you will, this story informs readers of personality traits that lead people towards bankruptcy.

What about Singaporeans and public transportation? Our story continues with this love–hate relationship and in particular, Singaporeans' angst with public transportation. Using EZ-link data, our research findings very much reflect Swee Hoon's beef whenever her bus doesn't arrive as scheduled.

In Chapter 12, Teng's career-focused lady neighbour realises that playing the boys' game of golf can give her a leg up to corporate directorship. Intriguing?

Many of our research-driven stories are inspired by our personal experiences. The story on children nudging their parents to save energy was triggered by Sumit's constant accommodation to his little girl's requests. We find that it's difficult for parents to say "No" to their young children even on matters as mundane as utility conservation.

Another story on water conservation is loosely based on one of the author's daughter who takes an inordinate amount of time to have her shower.

The story culminates with the financial challenges Teng's parents face upon retirement. It isn't golden spending in silver years. How then do retirees adapt when they have so much free time with little cash coming in?

Such day-to-day issues resonate with Singaporeans from all walks of life. We try to incorporate as many as our research covers — issues that those living in Singapore would want to know.

Other interesting issues woven in this book include how the Goods and Services Tax pushes Teng and his wife to shop in Johor and how this affects their savings and Singapore businesses; how his wife and her friends change their shopping habits during the Great Singapore Sale; how the haze or a nearby construction site affects Teng's water and electricity consumption; and how merely giving instant feedback on water consumption encourages his neighbours to save.

We hope reading this book enables readers to not only have economic insights to their daily issues but also develop a deeper appreciation for research. Enjoy!

CHAPTER 1

Dragon Babies, There Are So Many of You

It was at the crack of dawn when the first jab of pain came. "Could this be it?" the first-time mum wondered, a quizzical look panning across her face. Her heart skipped a beat. Perhaps she had overeaten. After all, she did have a heavy dinner the evening before — hard-boiled egg with pork belly and *toufu* braised in dark soya sauce.

The contractions came again. This time, Moi was more certain. The bundle of joy that she and Hong had been looking forward to would soon be here. Both anxiety and joy flitted and danced in her heart.

Having a baby was a carefully planned affair. Their firstborn had to be a Dragon baby. After all, according to the Chinese zodiac, the year of the Dragon is especially fortunate for babies, marriages and businesses. Those born as Dragons are believed to be smart, lucky and magnanimous.

For this family in particular, having a Dragon baby was not only auspicious for the child but also for the father. According to the fortune

[A]ccording to the Chinese zodiac, the year of the Dragon is especially fortunate for babies, marriages and businesses. Those born as Dragons are believed to be smart, lucky and magnanimous.

teller at the wet market, a baby born the following year, which would be a Snake, wouldn't get along well with Hong. Their personalities would *qiong* (meaning 'clash'). If Moi didn't have a baby that year, she would have to wait for another five years for a child to be compatible with Hong's zodiac sign. That would be too long a wait.

And the scan had shown it would be a boy. How propitious! The grandparents from both sides would be thrilled to have a Dragon grandson. Especially Hong's parents. He would be the first grandchild for Ah Kong and Ah Mah (meaning 'grandfather' and 'grandmother' respectively).

Hong and Moi didn't want to name their son Leng or Loong (meaning 'dragon'). There would be many boys born that year called that. They wanted their son to be special and not one of many. Instead, they named him Teng (腾 meaning 'to fly, rise, soaring like a dragon' and suggestive of a bright future).

And so it was. Teng came into this world with feisty cries. Ah Mah said that meant Teng was ambitious.

Moi and Hong had become Ma and Pa.

Growing Up

Teng grew up feeling like a princeling. Not that the family was well to do. But being born in the year of the Dragon had, as one might expect, its benefits.

His father, a clerk, and his mother, a shop assistant at the hardware store near the market, doted on him — what he wanted was what he got. Nothing was too much for their precious Dragon son.

Ah Kong and Ah Mah showered gifts on him too and always gave him the benefit of the doubt whenever there were skirmishes between him and his siblings.

When it was time to register for a primary school, Ma and Pa found that getting into a good school was tougher than they had anticipated. Although they had read in the newspapers that there was a spike of some 8 percent in Dragon births compared to other years, they had misjudged the intensity of competition for school places. After all, the government did announce that to cater for the larger number of incoming Primary One students, they had opened additional new primary schools.

The newspapers had even writeups on the number of births in Singapore for each of the Chinese zodiac animal years and there was always a spike when it came to the year of the Dragon.

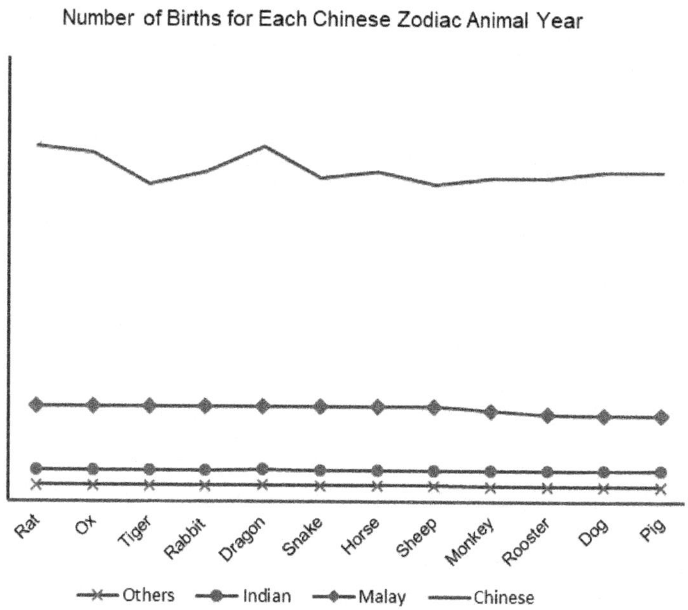

Teng went to a school within walking distance from his three-room HDB (Housing & Development Board) flat in Jurong. Not the best school in the neighbourhood, but the 200-metre distance meant that Teng could walk there on his own, not to mention the extra snooze he got compared to friends who lived farther away. And that short, leisurely walk stirred his interest in cars.

While the flats surrounding him seemed monotonously homogenous with no distinctive feature, the myriad of cars zooming by as Teng walked to school fascinated him, adding a spring to each of Teng's steps.

Class sizes in his cohort were a little larger than usual to accommodate the Dragon babies. And more often than not, like Teng, his classmates were spoilt for choice by over-indulgent parents and grandparents.

Competition was stiff too. Teng had just mastered spelling and writing his full name in both English and Chinese. He thought it was an achievement, judging by the encouragement he received from Ah Mah, Ah Kong, Ma and Pa. But amongst his peers, it seemed to be anything but that.

During the first week of school, his form teacher was already reeling off her list of expectations — all homework must be handed in on time, multiplication tables must be memorised, each child was expected to read at least one English and one Chinese story book a week. The list went on.

To top it off, his form teacher would write on the side of the blackboard two sets of names — the names written in white chalk were the top three students who excelled in spelling; those written in red chalk were those who fared poorly. And with 45 students in the class, more than the usual size of 40, it was even harder to be in the top three.

Competition was everything. Some of his classmates were competitive on all fronts — they fought to be the first to raise their hand to answer a question; jostled to get the best seat when the teacher called the class to come forward during story time; and strived to be on the better team when it came to PE (Physical Education). They had their game face on at all times.

He remembered when Ma accompanied him to school to buy his textbooks. He didn't understand why Ma wanted two sets of books. There was only one of him – why two books each for Chinese, English, Maths and even Music?

It turned out that many parents were *kiasu* (meaning 'scared to lose'). They had bought two sets so that one could be kept in school, while the other was kept at home for self-study or for private tutors.

So even though they came from a humble background, Ma and Pa would spend less on themselves to make sure that Teng was not put at a disadvantage.

There were some 43,000 Dragon babies born that year and apparently, the textbook publisher had printed 50,000 copies, thinking it was more than enough. They had misjudged. Most of the parents were clamouring to buy more – the books were soon out of stock.

Teng had never felt such intense pressure before. After all, he had always been the favoured child and the thought that others were just as special as he was, was just quite discouraging.

The Cohort Size Effect

Once, Teng and his best friend Peter were comparing their largesse from Lunar New Year. They had amassed quite a large sum of money from their *hong baos* (meaning 'red packets').

"Teng, why study so hard?" lamented a naïve Peter in Singlish or Singapore's English. "Born in the year of Dragon can give so much headache. So many Dragon babies. There's so much competition.

I think just collecting *hong bao* is good enough. Aunties, uncles, grandfather, grandmother — they can give *hong bao* every year and we're set for life."

"Why are you complaining? Competition is good," responded Teng.

"I thought so too. But that day, I saw someone on TV say something called the 'kor-hot' size effect or something like that. What a very *cheem* (meaning 'difficult') word," said Peter, scratching his head. "Something like the more people there are in one age group, the harder it is to get a job or do well. And the man on TV said Dragon people suffer from this."

"Hah? Got like that one meh?" exclaimed Teng, as he sat up straight on hearing this.

He had always been told by Ah Mah that as a Dragon baby, he would always be blessed with good fortune, and that life would be smooth sailing. So what is this about not doing well?

Teng never had problems with money. What he wanted, his parents provided, especially since he had been diagnosed with asthma. On the days the air got a little bit hazy, Teng would be wheezing away with an itchy nose. But the doctor had reassured Ma that he would probably outgrow his asthma.

Once, he had gone to a scouts' campfire event at a school in the Bukit Timah area. He drooled as he saw the fleet of polished Mercedes-Benzes and BMWs waiting to pick up the kids. Wouldn't it be nice to be chauffeured around in a spanking new set of wheels and show it off to his friends?

Another time, after Ah Mah had bought his favourite Van Houten almond chocolates, he had proudly boasted to her, "Ah Mah, next time when I grow up, I will become my own boss. Then, I will *blanjah* (meaning 'treat') you to the best restaurant in Singapore."

Yes, Teng had dreams of making it big.

Now this 'kor-hot' size effect may well dash his big dreams. Where is the good fortune he was supposed to have? Teng was puzzled and troubled.

"Let's go ask Miss Aishah. Maybe she knows what 'kor-hot' means," he suggested to Peter.

Miss Aishah Explains

Miss Aishah was their English teacher. And their favourite too. Not only was she pretty, she was also young — unlike the old draconian Science teacher the boys had.

Pleasantly surprised at the two rambunctious boys' question, she explained, "Ah . . . I know what you mean, Peter. That was the study reported on Channel 5 News the other evening.

"Spelt C-O-H-O-R-T, 'cohort' means the group of people similar to you — for example in age. So you can say that people born in the year of the Dragon, like you, belong to the same cohort."

"So that means we have a big cohort lah, since got so many of us Dragon babies?" interrupted Peter eagerly. He tried to speak in better English but the truth of the matter was everyone in his family and almost all the students in school spoke Singlish.

"Yes, the Dragon year babies belong to a larger cohort than, say, those born in the year of the Tiger, which usually see fewer births," explained Miss Aishah.

"But why big cohort means we suffer?" interjected Teng anxiously.

Getting a little annoyed at the frequent interruption, Miss Aishah sat both boys down and explained to them what she had heard over the TV News and read in the newspapers.

"Research has shown that as cohort size increases, there is lower productivity and wages. Unemployment is also higher. People from larger cohorts are also more likely to commit crime. They tend to form higher material aspirations during childhood. But because opportunities are limited, there is a gap between aspiration and reality. Does this make sense to you?"

[A]s cohort size increases, there is lower productivity and wages. Unemployment is also higher. People from larger cohorts are also more likely to commit crime. They tend to form higher material aspirations during childhood.

"You mean we have big dreams. And being Dragon babies, even bigger dreams. But because there are so many of us, and opportunities are fewer, more will be disappointed?" Teng asked, trying to put what Miss Aishah had said in the kind of English he understood.

"Yes, you've gotten it right," smiled Miss Aishah. She continued, "That news report was from a study done by a group of professors from the National University of Singapore (NUS). They studied people born in the year of Dragon as well as those born in other years.

"They found that the number of Chinese births is 8.4 percent higher in Dragon years and 7.3 percent lower in Tiger years. You know why, right? Chinese parents like their children to be born in the year of the Dragon because it means good luck, while babies born in the year of the Tiger, especially females, may be too fierce. So they want babies in the Dragon year but not in the Tiger year.

"That is why when schools are admitting children born in the Dragon year, we have to open more classes to cater for the larger intake.

"Do you want to know more about what the professors found?" asked Miss Aishah.

The boys nodded their heads eagerly.

Education and Salary

Miss Aishah continued, "The professors were very detailed in their research. They collected data from people entering the local universities, as well as birth, financial and property data from different sources. They also searched bankruptcy records.

"They were also mindful that Singaporean men had to do National Service and enter the university two years after girls born in the same year.

"After accounting for this, the profs found that as a cohort, people born in the year of the Dragon had lower admission scores than people born in other years. This means they are about 3 percent less likely to be admitted to the university than people born in other years."

"But why? We are supposed to be smart and lucky," fumed an upset Peter, agitated at this bad news.

"Well," explained Miss Aishah, "the professors explained that there are at least two possible reasons. The first is what they call *selection effects*. This means that perhaps families from lower socioeconomic backgrounds, with poorer financial management skills, are more likely to practise zodiac birth timing. And such family circumstances might put their Dragon babies at a disadvantage. But the NUS professors found little evidence of this."

"Oh! Then what is the reason?" asked the boys anxiously.

[T]here is a lower quality of pre-tertiary education due to larger cohort sizes.

"Instead, there is another explanation — that is, perhaps there is a lower quality of pre-tertiary education due to larger cohort sizes. The profs actually found this explanation to be more likely.

Peter and Teng stared widely at Miss Aishah and nodded their heads, mesmerised by what she had to say about the professors' findings. They wanted to know why they were at a disadvantage. The irony did not escape them.

"Remember, we have the two-year compulsory National Service for Singaporean males. So, men are two years older than females of their birth cohort when they enter university and their first job.

"Now, although Dragon men and women share similar early life environments, Dragon men enter the university and the job market not with Dragon women but with women who are two years younger, those born in the year of the Horse. On the other hand, Dragon women start working with men who are two years older, men born in the year of the Tiger.

"As the cohort size for Dragon babies increases, the ratio of younger Dragon women to older men increases. So for Dragon women, they are less likely to find a high quality marriage match as there are relatively fewer Tiger men in the same tertiary year as they are, or they may take longer to do so.

"By the same reasoning, Horse women benefit from the larger supply of older men from the Dragon cohort. You follow so far?"

The two boys weren't sure, but like typical Singaporeans who didn't dare to contradict, especially someone in authority, they simply nodded.

Miss Aishah continued. "If there is a cohort size effect, then Dragon men and Horse women who entered the university and the job market at the same time will earn lower salaries.

"Dragon women will also be at a disadvantage because there are so many of them that year.

"However, Horse men who entered the university and joined the workforce after the Dragon men and women should earn an average salary because they belong to a smaller cohort. Understand? So far so good?"

When Miss Aishah saw that both boys were still attentive and seemingly digesting what she had said, she continued.

"Well, not good news for you two, I'm afraid. The professors found cohort size effects. As I said earlier, Dragon babies have lower odds of admission to a local university. And not only that, they found that Dragon men earned about 2 to 6 percent lower income, while Dragon and Horse women graduates earned about 3 to 9 percent lower income. But for Horse male graduates their income was the average, not affected because they were not part of a larger cohort. So these differences in income were due to cohort size."

Dragon men earned about 2 to 6 percent lower income, while Dragon and Horse women graduates earned about 3 to 9 percent lower income. But for Horse male graduates their income was the average, not affected because they were not part of a larger cohort.

"Hah? What happened?" Teng cried in disbelief.

"Maybe knowing more about the findings will help you understand and prepare for the future," said Miss Aishah.

Finances and Consumption

She continued, "The professors also had financial data on how people spent on their credit and debit cards, how much they saved, where they lived and so on. Given their dates of birth, the researchers knew who were born in the year of the Dragon. The good news is that they found people born in the Dragon year were not bigger risk takers nor were they more likely to become embroiled in bankruptcies or lawsuits."

"There you go!" cheered Peter at the first sign that Dragon babies were not faring too badly after all.

"Hold your horses!" laughed Miss Aishah, "Pardon the pun. So funny, horses and Horse women and men. Sorry, I'm an English teacher."

The boys didn't get the joke but Miss Aishah continued anyway.

"What is disconcerting is that despite their lower incomes, both Dragon men and women were more materialistic. They like to show off. They spend more on 'visible' items such as clothes, watches, jewellery, home furnishings and appliances.

"They spend something like 6 to 11 percent more than others. And among the younger Dragon people, the professors found that they spend even more than older Dragon people. So, you guys had better not be a spendthrift. You have to be more careful with your money."

"Aiyoh! Die lah like that," Peter interjected, crestfallen. His joy had been short-lived. "Looks like it's a curse on the Dragon!"

Miss Aishah tried to keep the two boys in line by continuing. "Besides the more conspicuous items, Dragon babies are also more likely to own a private condominium, which is another status symbol. So why do you think Dragon people spend more on buying these flashy things?"

"I know, I know," shouted the high-strung Peter. "Since you say Dragon babies have less chance to go to university, then maybe they are also not very good at saving money. So they anyhow spend. And then, maybe they also feel a bit awkward because of lower level of education. So they buy branded handbags and watches to show like they are the king — in control of things."

"Hmm . . . possibly," replied Miss Aishah. "But then, how do you explain the Horse women? They also have lower incomes but they spend *less* rather than more. Remember, they were in the same cohort as the Dragon men when they graduated. And that was a large cohort."

Teng, who had been keeping quite quiet, was thoughtful. Then he spoke.

"Miss Aishah, is it because our family has always been telling us that Dragon people are always lucky and so Dragon people believe it themselves. They become overly optimistic when it comes to money matters and so they just spend and spend?"

"Possibly," replied Miss Aishah, "but if that were the case, Dragon people would also spend more on less conspicuous items, right? 'Spend and spend' means spend on everything, not just on brand name or visible items. But the professors did not find that. Dragon people spend more, but only on materialistic items, not all items."

Both boys scratched their heads. What Miss Aishah said sounded logical but how can one account for the findings?

Seeing their puzzled looks, Miss Aishah said, "Let me explain what the professors thought was the rationale behind the Dragon people's conspicuous consumption, even though they earn less.

"The NUS profs thought that people born in the year of the Dragon understand that these cultural beliefs are not true, but they value the boost in self-image by being associated with this auspicious zodiac animal. So they become more self-confident. To maintain such self-confidence and think positively about themselves, they have to convince others of their value. So they are willing to incur more to buy these expensive items to make themselves feel good."

[P]eople born in the year of the Dragon ... value the boost in self-image by being associated with this auspicious zodiac animal.... To maintain such self-confidence and think positively about themselves, ... they are willing to incur more to buy these expensive items to make themselves feel good.

"Wah! So deep!" laughed Peter. "Actually, I think it describes me quite well."

"I'm so glad you boys understand," said Miss Aishah appreciatively.

"Now, if the NUS professors were here and you could ask them questions, what would you be interested in knowing?" Miss Aishah asked as she tried to prod the boys to think more about issues that might interest them.

The boys thought for a while.

"Well, I'm the firstborn in my family. I have one sister and one brother," Teng volunteered. "I wonder whether the professors have considered position in the family. Would the firstborn Dragon have more stress than a Dragon baby who is the youngest child?

"Or forget everything about Chinese zodiac sign. I would like to know whether being the only child or the eldest or the youngest matters. Do we do less well in our studies? Do we spend more? I heard from my Ma that last time, the Singapore government wanted people to have no more than two children. But now, they encourage people to have more. So if there are three children in the family, how is the eldest child in the family different from the single child who is also the eldest?"

"Ahh . . . So there are a few issues here," said Miss Aishah as she distilled Teng's thoughts. "First is position of the Dragon baby in the family. Does being the firstborn Dragon child or youngest born Dragon child affect a child's performance? Second is family size. Does having only one child, two children or three children affect a child's performance? And third is the child's position in the family. Does being the eldest child, second child or youngest child affect your performance?"

Peter couldn't wait to express himself.

"For me, I think I will ask the professors whether Dragon parents tend to have Dragon babies. Or maybe parents who are not Dragons want to have Dragon babies to make up for not being a Dragon themselves. But I think now we are quite modern, not so traditional anymore. So maybe, this Dragon baby effect is more likely to occur among parents who are more of the Chinese religious type. I don't know how to say it . . . you know, may be like the Taoists but not the Christians."

"Ahh . . . Let me rephrase it for you," said Miss Aishah as she smiled at how the two boys were coming up with ideas of their own. "You are interested to know whether Dragon or non-Dragon parents are more likely to have Dragon babies. And you think non-Dragon parents would prefer Dragon babies more so than Dragon parents. Perhaps Dragon parents know the cohort size effects from their experience and do not wish for the same to happen to their children. But non-Dragon parents do not know any better. And if there is a difference, you think it is probably due to religion, where parents who believe in the Chinese zodiac will want Dragon babies more so than those who believe less in the Chinese horoscope. Did I get it right?"

And the two boys just smiled, a young boys' crush on their favourite teacher.

WANT TO KNOW MORE?

This chapter is based on Sumit Agarwal, Qian Wenlan, Sing Tien Foo and Tan Poh Lin, "Dragon Babies: Fortunes of Birth and Life Outcomes," (January 2017). Working Paper, National University of Singapore; and Sumit Agarwal and Qian Wenlan, "Dragon Babies, Muted Achievements," *The Straits Times*, (27 January 2017). http://www.straitstimes.com/opinion/dragon-babies-muted-achievements

CHAPTER 2

Taxi Driver, Where Are You?

Eventually, it came to be that Teng and his friends did not fare too well in school. Some called it a self-fulfilling prophecy as borne by the research findings on cohort size effects. Others said that it was expected – after all, Dragon babies are spoilt stiff. As a Dragon baby, Teng had high aspirations. But as the years went by, his world view became more realistic – he came to recognise that he was not the centre of the universe.

Nevertheless, Teng loved to enjoy life and basked in it. During his days in primary school, he was caught up with the popular game of marbles. Cheered on by fellow schoolmates, the challenge often reached a high – much like cock fights. The winner of each game took all the marbles home.

Teng's bagful of marbles, bought by Ma, was upgraded as he painstakingly honed his marble skills and won game after game. He became the envy among his friends. But that fame came at the expense of his studies, much to his parents' dismay.

He was particularly proud of his most prized possession: the glass marble ball with specks of brilliant gold that gleamed under the sun. He basked in the "oohs" and "ahhs" of his friends as he drew the marble from his bag ever so slowly – milking every bit of admiration he could get. He just loved the attention.

Years later, one of his friends sneaked the latest handheld Nintendo Game Boy to school. Teng badly wanted one too. While Ma and Pa had turned his request down as they were not too pleased with his below-par grades, he knew all too well from experience that his request would come to pass.

Teng knew how to wrap his parents around his finger. This had never failed: "Ma, Pa. I promise I will be more hardworking. I will pay more attention in class. I will do my homework immediately after coming home." With his well-practiced earnest look, Ma would relent and persuade Pa to give him another chance. After all, as their eldest son, they wanted him to be happy.

But his dismal academic performance appeared to put an early end to such luxuries. Ma and Pa could not be supporting him all the time.

First Job

Armed with a less-than-stellar 'O' level certificate, Teng explored his limited employment options. Peter – a chatty boy with more friends than Teng could count – did not fare too well either and wasn't keen on pursuing further studies.

Teng's early passion in cars fuelled his job search. He had salivated at the posh cars he saw at the elite schools in Bukit Timah. He recalled how, as he walked to school, he would test whether he could recognise the make of a car from afar just by its shape. Teng felt he would be happy working in the car business.

He eventually went into the car business, beginning as an apprentice with a car repair shop next to a petrol station. While tinkering with car parts, Teng often dreamed of the day he could drive a car, like the Mercedes-Benzes or BMWs he saw at the Bukit Timah school – wouldn't that be cool? He and Peter could then arrive in style at their favourite watering hole in Chinatown. Going to Changi Point for their occasional fishing trips would be a breeze too.

Some years into working, Teng met Siew Ling. Six years his junior, she was quietly sophisticated, easy to please and with an eye for fashion. Protective and somewhat traditional, she was the complete opposite to Teng's fiery temper and impetuous need for instant gratification. In a strange way, the stark difference was complementary and added a comforting stability to the relationship, something which Teng found unexplainably reassuring.

Teng and Siew Ling dated for a while. Siew Ling loved going to the movies, a favourite pastime among Singaporeans before the Internet became the rage. She enjoyed the special effects and magic in the Harry Potter movies, and relished the acrobatic fighting moves and comedy acts by Jackie Chan in *Rush Hour* and *Police Story*. Teng would just sit back and watch her laugh. That was enough to make him happy.

But the mechanic job was not going anywhere. With the repair shop under-staffed, tempers flared whenever repair jobs stacked up. This was not helped by the fact that finding mechanical faults in old cars was more challenging than finding Waldo or Wally in the popular children's book.

Going out with Siew Ling with remnant grease under his fingernails and sometimes even on his clothes was not ideal. Teng was ever so conscious whenever he held Siew Ling's hand with his own less-than-grease-free hand. Though Siew Ling didn't mind, Teng felt that Siew

Ling was a princess who deserved the best. Moreover, the lingering grease smell was a constant reminder of his unfulfilling mechanical job.

Taxi Driving

After more than a decade of repairing cars, Teng decided to try another line of work.

He had heard from his customers that whenever they had to take a cab after dropping off their car for repair, the taxis were nowhere to be found especially during peak hours and shift-changing times. Having earlier obtained his driver's license, Teng explored taxi driving as a possible career.

Despite having one of the highest cab densities in the world with about 5,500 taxis per 1 million people compared to 1,522 in New York and 3,285 in London, and with cab services relatively inexpensive (where a 10-kilometre trip costs approximately $10, which is much less than the $22 fare for the same trip taken in New York), it can be difficult to hail a cab.

Despite having one of the highest cab densities in the world with about 5,500 taxis per 1 million people compared to 1,522 in New York and 3,285 in London, and with cab services relatively inexpensive (where a 10-kilometre trip costs approximately $10, which is much less than the $22 fare for the same trip taken in New York), it can be difficult to hail a cab.

Teng thought this would be a good opportunity to make better money as there is a constant demand for a taxi. Besides, taxi driving allowed him some flexibility; he would be able to choose when to pick up passengers, ferry his girlfriend (soon-to-be wife) around, and nap in between trips. Most importantly, the prospect of telling others that he would be driving a four-wheeled vehicle (short of realising his dream of owning a car) was enticing.

And so Teng became a taxi driver at 30.

He had a relief driver — a friend living in the same block. Teng took the morning shift, hitting the road by 5 am. Over time, Teng learned where he should ply for easy pickups, especially when starting off from his home. He usually found customers in the housing estates where there were always people needing a cab for work. Thereafter, his routes were determined by passengers' destinations.

Much to Teng's surprise, he would often break even by 10 am, earning enough to cover his share of the day's taxi rental and diesel. Thereafter, he would be earning profits.

Compared to his back-breaking sweaty job as a mechanic, driving an air-conditioned taxi seemed a breeze except for being cooped up inside a confined environment for long periods breathing the taxi's stale air. Other challenges he faced included the daily managing of coins and dollar notes in various small denominations, as well as the constant reminder to top up the cash card in his IU (In-vehicle Unit) to at least $20 for CBD (Central Business District) and ERP (Electronic Road Pricing) charges. Teng also needed a big bottle of water to keep him refreshed.

Learning the Ropes

During one of his breaks, Teng chatted with a couple of senior cab drivers hanging around Tiong Bahru market. They were musing over how they were going to spend the rest of the day.

"My mother got an appointment at the polyclinic. So after lunch, I'm going home and call it a day," said one driver.

"You met your target already or not?" asked the other.

"Met already. So now can relax. You leh?"

"Not yet. Got to drive for four more hours."

Out of curiosity, Teng interjected and asked, "Excuse me, I'm a new driver. Can I ask how you set targets? Can you teach me please?"

"Up to you lor," said the first driver. "You can set by the hour or by income."

"Yah. Like for me, I set by the hour. I have a relief driver. In the 12 hours I have the taxi, I'm on the road driving for about six to seven hours. Don't count breaks and pee stops. Of the six–seven hours, for about four hours I have passengers to drive around, the other two to three hours I look for passengers. When I have driven for about seven hours, I stop."

"Your estimated seven hours do not include toilet and meal breaks, right?" Teng clarified.

"Yup, the seven hours don't count pee breaks. You can't drive continuously for seven hours. *Makan* (meaning 'eat') and pee stops take up may be another two hours. So in total, counting driving and break stops, it's about nine to 10 hours. So let's say I start at 6 am. Then I stop at about 3 pm. If I start later, I stop later lah. Then for the rest of the time, the taxi is parked downstairs of my block."

"Oh I see . . . You don't go by takings?" Teng asked.

"You can if you want to. One of my friends goes by income. His costs are about $120 for rental and $40 for diesel – plus or minus. He wants to earn $100 net a day. When he reaches his target, he stops. So for example, he makes $260, minus costs he gets $100, then he stops. If it's a good day, he can get $260 in five or six hours in the morning. Then he says goodbye, goes home and rests. If it's a lousy day, he continues driving lor. Drive and drive until he gets $260."

"So it's up to you," chimed in the second driver. "But once you hit your target – whether by hours or by takings – you can relax already. There's no need to be on the road anymore. Also very few want to drive in the evening because they are tired lah. We want to be with the family."

"Worse still if it's raining. You don't want to get into accidents. And raining means higher chance of accidents. You better watch out. When *kena* (meaning 'have') accident, you have to pay the first $2,000 towards accident claims. Not worth it lah. So it's better not to drive when it's raining heavily even though there are so many people wanting a taxi," added the first senior driver.

"In fact, I remember ComfortDelgro coming up with a report about road accidents. You know, ComfortDelgro got two types of taxis, right? Yellow if you drive CityCab and blue if you drive Comfort. So they got these university professors to study which colour is safer for taxi drivers."

"I think I got the report in my taxi. I'll go and get it," said the second senior driver. Off he went, leaving Teng and his friend to carry on with their conversation.

"Huh? What do you mean 'safer'?" asked Teng for clarification.

"Let me explain. You want to get passengers, right?" asked the first senior cab driver.

Teng nodded.

"Yellow is supposed to be the most noticeable colour. So in America, a lot of taxis are yellow because people can easily spot a yellow taxi. Then it becomes easier to get passengers.

"So if spotting a yellow taxi helps to bring in passengers, can yellow also be used to avoid *langah* (meaning 'collision')? After all, other users of the road should be able to spot a yellow taxi too."

[Y]ellow taxis have 6.1 fewer accidents per 1,000 taxis per month than blue taxis. That means if you drive a yellow taxi, the chances of you meeting an accident are 9 percent less than if you drive a blue taxi.

"Hmm . . . That makes sense," said Teng. "So what did they find?"

"The professors found that yellow taxis have 6.1 fewer accidents per 1,000 taxis per month than blue taxis. That means if you drive a yellow taxi, the chances of you meeting an accident are 9 percent less than if you drive a blue taxi," explained the first senior driver.

Just then, the second senior driver returned with the report in his hand. It was a leaflet with one page devoted to the study.

"Really, yellow taxis have lower accidents than blue taxis," said the taxi driver pointing to a chart in the brochure. "For every 1,000 taxis, there are 65.6 accidents each month for yellow taxis compared to 71.7 for blue taxis. *Heng* ah (meaning 'thank goodness'). I drive a yellow taxi."

"Oh no! Mine's blue," thought Teng. "Don't tell me this stupid Dragon curse is still here," Teng wondered as he remembered what Miss Aishah had explained about cohort size effect.

"Hey, look. There're more details. Yellow taxis have less accidents when it is dark with street lighting than in the day when there's daylight. Why ah?" asked Teng.

"Like what I said earlier. Yellow is a brighter, more noticeable colour. Street lighting makes yellow more outstanding than blue because the sky is dark. Yellow pops up more than blue especially when it's dark. But in the day, the contrast for yellow and blue is almost same same. So yellow really helps when driving in the early morning or at night," explained the first senior driver.

"So I'd better be more careful since mine is a blue taxi. *Kam sia* (meaning 'thank you') for helping me," Teng said as he waved goodbye to his fellow cab drivers.

Siew Ling's Taxi Superstitions

When Teng met Siew Ling for their next date, he told her his concerns of driving a blue taxi, instead of a yellow one, and the accident rates.

Siew Ling, somewhat superstitious especially when it involved someone dear to her, was not taking any chances. She scoured the Waterloo Street area where there were several shops selling Chinese religious charms. She bought a dangling charm with crystals that Teng could hang on his front view mirror. The shopkeeper had told her that the crystals could reflect light to ward off evil spirits.

But being *kiasu*, she also bought mini statuettes of not one, but three gods, which were to be placed on the dashboard: the Goddess of Mercy or *Guanyin* to protect Teng from any traffic accidents; the Jade Emperor or *Shangti* – the supreme god of law and order – to bring justice and protect her innocent Teng in the rare possibility that the goddess could not prevent the unfortunate event from occurring as well as potential traffic police cases; and, Buddha for additional protection.

Seeing Siew Ling's enthusiasm in buying these charms, the shopkeeper suggested a *yin yang* amulet that Teng could put in his wallet for protection and good luck. A *yin yang* amulet has dark and light patterned swirls to reflect Taoist belief in complementary forces.

As a result of superstitious beliefs, Teng's taxi, like many other taxis, was adorned with a multitude of religious charms. The mix of gods from Taoism and Buddhism displayed on his dashboard reflected the Singaporean Chinese religious culture that combined and sometimes confused the two religions most commonly associated with the Chinese.

The Taxi Dilemma

Being a taxi driver himself and knowing how some of his fellow cab drivers spent their time on the road, Teng pondered on his parents' complaints about not being able to find a cab when they needed one.

On one occasion, he recalled Ma and Pa coming home very late for dinner. Ma, the more vociferous of the two, was fuming that it would have been faster taking the bus than the taxi. They had visited a relative in Pasir Ris. Instead of taking the bus to the MRT (Mass Rapid Transit) station and then boarding the train, followed by another bus to reach home, Ma and Pa thought a taxi ride would be more convenient and faster.

They were wrong. After waiting for some 20 minutes, they were still standing by the roadside under Singapore's sweltering heat. It was almost impossible to find a cab that was willing to bring them back to their flat in Jurong. They then recalled reading newspaper reports of taxi drivers lamenting that it was difficult to eke out a decent living. This stark contradiction between what they had read and what they had experienced was puzzling.

With this recollection vivid in his mind, Teng wondered whether he should be like the cab drivers he met — that is to stop work upon reaching their target or to take the high road and work till the handover to his co-driver. This decision had always perplexed him.

Professor Agarwal

Teng was driving along Farrer Road one late morning. It had been a fruitful morning. He had managed to pick up several passengers earlier and his takings had already covered his taxi rental and diesel costs for that day.

A man hailed him from the Empress Road market. The passenger wanted to go to the National University of Singapore at Clementi.

Slightly built, the Indian passenger started conversing with Teng about the type of passengers he had ferried.

"I've had all kinds. And I've learnt to figure out which country they come from by their accents. Those from China tend to talk so loudly – though I must admit, there are some who are very sweet and polite. Those from Hong Kong have a strong Cantonese-accented English. Thais have a sing-song accent. Indonesians are a little tougher to identify because some speak very much like a Westerner while others speak with a Malay accent."

Then, his passenger began asking him many questions about his taxi driving habits.

"Strange," thought Teng. But not wanting to sound impolite, Teng answered as best as he could.

The conversation was long enough for Teng to learn that the passenger was a professor in finance and economics. He had come to Singapore from the United States and was interested in studying taxi drivers. The professor was curious why he, like Teng's parents, could not find a cab at times despite Singapore having more taxis per resident vis-à-vis most other countries.

It turned out that Professor Agarwal had studied the minute-by-minute trip history of over 10,000 cabs furnished with the Global Positioning System (GPS) satellite-based tracking and dispatching system installed in all Singapore cabs. Within one month of trip history, he had 520 million data points to study.

"Let's think in terms of a taxi vehicle, not in terms of a driver, as there may be shifts between the main and relief drivers. My colleagues and I found that in a day, a typical cab has a passenger on board for about seven to eight hours, earning on average $25 an hour; it is free and looking for passengers for four to five hours; break times take up about four hours; and it is offline – probably the driver is sleeping or doing personal errands — for the remaining seven to eight hours," offered Professor Agarwal. "How interesting," thought Teng. "I wonder whether I was one of the drivers studied." Aloud he asked, "Professor, were you the one who studied whether yellow or blue cabs are safer?"

[I]n a day, a typical cab has a passenger on board for about seven to eight hours, earning on average $25 an hour; it is free and looking for passengers for four to five hours; break times for the driver take up about four hours ...

"Oh! You've heard of that study," said Professor Agarwal, pleasantly surprised that the taxi driver had heard of the research. "No, that was done by my colleagues at the NUS Business School. We are all interested in taxi drivers. You guys are interesting to study!

"I know you are driving and your eyes should be on the road. So, let me leave a copy of my research summary with you. You can read it when you are free," said Professor Agarwal as he placed a two-page sheet on the front passenger's seat. "The summary is easy to understand. It has lots of graphs."

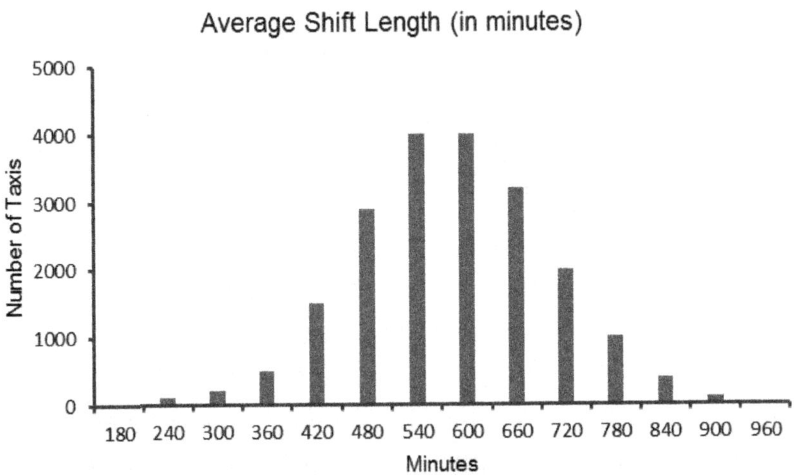

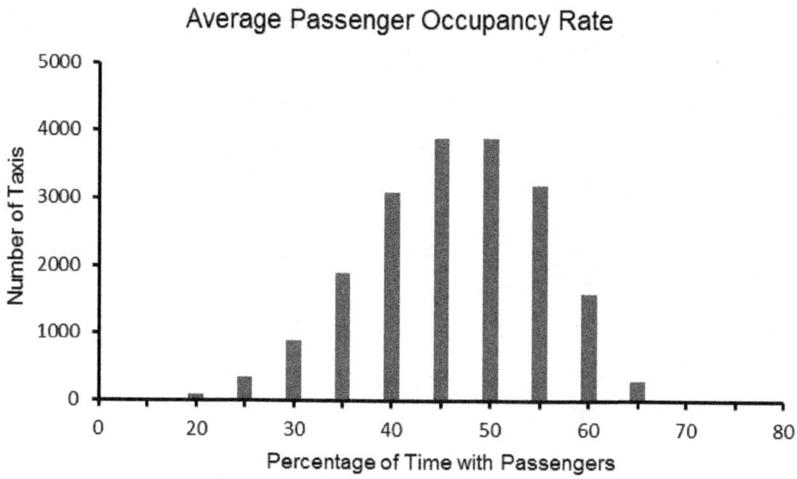

At a traffic light, Teng took a quick glance at the research summary placed next to him and saw two graphs — one on the average time drivers spend on a shift and the other on the average frequency that a taxi is occupied with a passenger.

Professor Agarwal noticed Teng's swift attention on the graph showing the average occupancy. "Ahh . . . A bread and butter issue," he thought.

He then voluntarily explained to Teng, "That graph shows the frequency in which a taxi is carrying a passenger.

"On average, a taxi driver spends less than 50 percent of the time with a passenger during a given shift. A small number of drivers are very good and have a passenger on board for over 70 percent of the shift time. But there is also a small group of drivers who have a passenger on board only 20 percent of the shift time. I hope you have many passengers."

"Thanks. I've learned where to pick up passengers. So far, touch wood, I'm doing ok," was Teng's response.

"That's good. We found that taxi drivers tend to stop work when they have reached their earnings and hours targets. When that happens,

[T]axi drivers tend to stop work when they have reached their earnings and hours targets. When that happens, taxis are under-utilised for some seven to eight hours a day.

taxis are under-utilised for some seven to eight hours a day. That's why I can't find a cab when I want to. You guys have already made enough money for the day," laughed Professor Agarwal.

To some degree, Teng wasn't too surprised that the professor confirmed what he had already suspected – many cab drivers he knew called it a day upon achieving their targets, whether in hours or income.

"And it's even worse when it's raining," Professor Agarwal continued with a sense of exasperation. "Singapore being a tropical country, has 178 rainy days a year. Some days, it rains more and some days, less. But I can't find you guys when I need you most."

But what astounded Teng was what the professor said next.

"You know what? This is the scary part – it's not just that taxi drivers stop driving once they reach their targets," said Professor Agarwal animatedly. "They are also quite short term in their planning."

"Short term? What does that mean?" Teng thought. But he didn't dare ask the professor.

Sensing that Teng was a bit confused by this, the professor explained.

"'Short term' means thinking about one day at a time, and not thinking about tomorrow or the day after or even how what happened the day before can affect the future.

"We found that regardless of whether taxi drivers experience more or fewer takings the previous day, they will revert to their usual daily income target in each of the following two days.

"It is surprising that how much they earned the day before does not affect their next day's target. If they made less on Day 1, they don't increase their income target on Day 2 to make up for the lower income the day before."

Teng was even more confused. He thought, "This professor sounds so knowledgeable. What he says is so *cheem*. It goes over my head. I don't understand."

"Professor, can you explain to me again, please?"

"Certainly. Suppose you earned only $100 yesterday when your target is $200. So you are short by $100. You would think that you would be more hardworking today to make up for yesterday's $100 shortfall, right? You would cut down on breaks and drive longer on the road, right?"

"Eh . . . I think so," said Teng hesitantly, as he himself wasn't sure what he would do in such a situation. He had never thought of it.

"But we didn't find that," said Professor Agarwal, shaking his head. "Instead, we found that the taxi driver behaves like normal. If his target is six hours of driving, he will stop at six hours regardless of how much he earned the day before. Or if his target is $200, he will stop when he hits $200 and not go for $250 to try to make up for the shortfall from the day before.

"The amount of time cab drivers spend on the road is not affected by whether they had a higher or a lower taking the previous day. Instead, it is determined largely by sticking to their daily targets — they seem to 'reboot' on a daily basis. I don't understand why. It just doesn't make financial sense."

The amount of time cab drivers spend on the road is not affected by whether they had a higher or a lower taking the previous day. Instead, it is determined largely by sticking to their daily targets — they seem to 'reboot' on a daily basis.

Thoughts raced quickly across Teng's mind, "If I don't make

enough the day before, I'll have to work harder the next day to make up for the shortfall. I must not forget about yesterday's takings and start from scratch."

His thoughts were interrupted as the professor continued talking.

"You know, it is worrisome to learn that cab drivers who do not achieve their daily targets do not try to work harder the next few days. They still have to pay the bills and provide food for the family. Household expenses remain the same. But if they continue like this, their long-term income will get lesser while their expenses remain the same or worse, with inflation, go up.

Thinking only of daily targets is very short term. Their personal household budgeting will be affected as they do not have a longer-term perspective.

"Thinking only of daily targets is very short term. Their personal household budgeting will be affected as they do not have a longer-term perspective."

After a pause the professor added with a sigh.

"Singapore is known to have a hardworking workforce. But to have taxi drivers stop working despite not earning enough the day before compromises the strong work ethic. It's quite sad."

Teng listened but didn't respond.

"What he said makes sense. I must make sure that I budget well and be hardworking in earning more money."

They were soon along Clementi Road heading towards the university. When they reached NUS Business School, Professor Agarwal gave some friendly advice, "Remember our conversation. I hope you'll do well."

"I hope so too, Prof.," thought Teng.

WANT TO KNOW MORE?

This chapter is based on Sumit Agarwal, Diao Mi, Jessica Pan and Sing Tien Foo, "Are Singaporeans Cabdrivers Target Earners?" (22 March 2015). Available at SSRN: https://ssrn.com/abstract=2338476 or http://dx.doi.org/10.2139/ssrn.2338476; and Ho Teck Hua, Chong Juin Kuan and Xia Xiaoyu, "Yellow Taxis have Fewer Accidents than Blue Taxis because Yellow is More Visible than Blue," *Proceedings of the National Academy of Sciences of the United States of America*, Vol. 114 (12), (2017), pp. 3074–3078.

CHAPTER 3

New Wife, New Life

Teng worked hard as a taxi driver. He wished he had directed that same amount of effort to his studies when he was younger. Perhaps life would have turned out a little easier.

From time to time when he was tempted to take a longer break or a day off like the other day when he had many 'On Call' bookings because of the rain, Teng was reminded of his conversation with the NUS professor who had advised him to keep his sights on the longer-term goal of prudent financial planning.

Being financially prudent was critical for Teng given that his profession as a taxi driver did not require him to make any CPF (Central Provident Fund) contribution. There were no forced savings plans that he had to contribute to — what he kept was all he had. Moreover, his legal status as a self-employed person meant that his taxi company was not mandated to make the employer contribution to his CPF account. Hence Teng, as a taxi driver, had no hidden savings such as CPF funds that he could count on to defray the cost of buying a flat or for retirement.

He needed to learn to exercise financial discipline.

Teng remembered a conversation between his Pa and Ma during the Asian financial crisis when Pa broke the news to Ma with a tinge of sadness and anxiety that Uncle Pheng and Uncle Beng had been retrenched. In fact, everyone's job was on the line when the crisis hit. Thankfully, Pa kept his job.

Growing up as a young working adult, Teng realised that one could be out of work even without an economic crisis.

His primary school classmate Muthu had worked for a brief period in a restaurant kitchen. Working in the kitchen was physically and mentally draining as it involved preparing food ingredients for long hours, followed by cooking under intense heat, fulfilling a high volume of customer orders correctly and promptly during the hectic dinner rush hour, and being berated by the boss occasionally.

With many eateries in Singapore, competition was tough. New restaurants were always popping up with exciting food menus. Moreover, food and beverage entrepreneurs had to face the fact that Singaporeans do not exhibit loyalty to any particular dish. Trying different and new cuisines is a favourite pastime among Singaporeans. It was not long before the restaurant Muthu was working at shut its doors. Muthu was out of a job.

Thankfully Siew Ling's job as a sales assistant at Good Fit shoe store was stable. Deemed boring in the eyes of some, it did not matter to her as the job matched her interest in fashion. Besides, she got to enjoy CPF contributions.

Over time, she and Teng thought they might have saved sufficiently to purchase their own home and proceeded to apply for a government-subsidised HDB flat. By that time, Teng was already above the average marriage age for Singaporean men. They often wondered about young couples who registered for a HDB flat early, in anticipation that they would have to wait for three to four years before getting one. The assumption, of course, was that the completion of the flat in a few years' time would coincide with the year they got married, allowing them to immediately settle in.

Yet, they had heard stories of young couples whose relationship didn't work out during the long wait for a flat. Did the long HDB waiting time make people commit to each other prematurely? Or was the long wait a blessing in disguise, for couples to have more time to assess each other before deciding to marry and finally retrieve the keys to their flat? They often wondered.

HDB Flats

The HDB was established in 1960 to develop affordable public housing and improve the quality of the living environment of Singaporeans. HDB flats or apartments are under temporary leaseholds for 99 years from the Singapore government. Originally intended for lower-income Singaporeans, grants are offered to first-time buyers for new flats bought directly from HDB, the quantum of which depends on income and size of the flat, among other considerations.

Over time with improving economic conditions, HDB began offering a variety of flat types and layouts suitable for various housing budgets. Three-room HDB flats come with two bedrooms and a joint living and dining room, while four- and five-room flats have three bedrooms (with five-room flats having an additional spare or study room). There are also two-room HDB flats for even more affordable housing and Executive Condominiums for more luxurious living.

Owners cannot sell the flat within the first five years. Thereafter, they can sell and buy from the resale market.

One of the criteria for grant eligibility when buying an HDB flat from the government is income. A couple's joint income must not exceed a ceiling. When Teng applied, it was $8,000.

Home Sweet Home

With financial constraints, Teng and Siew Ling compromised on the location of their first home. A centrally located flat would be out of their reach. The outskirts were more affordable.

Torn between Sengkang and Woodlands, they decided on the latter. They figured that Teng could always drive Siew Ling if she needed to go Orchard Road. And there's a Good Fit store at Woodlands Point which she could ask to be transferred to.

And to top it all, with Woodlands checkpoint close by, there was the possibility of shopping across the Causeway in Johor Bahru (JB).

The best they could afford was a three-bedroom HDB flat. Its 60 square metres came to a princely sum, exhausting all the little savings that Teng and Siew Ling had carefully amassed, and with a huge housing mortgage.

Upon moving in, friends congratulated them on their new flat. Teng would always laughed, "It still belongs to HDB."

Homebuyer Blues

There were homebuyer blues. Teng was worried that paying off the mortgage would be a burden on the newlyweds. They had never been in any debt before, let alone one so large. The monthly interest was staggering. He could not imagine paying so much each month just on interest alone.

Worrisome too is a potential threat to his taxi revenue. Teng had heard from fellow taxi drivers about a new form of shared-car driving in America that could affect the taxi-driving business. It had not come to Singapore yet but some of his friends were already talking about it.

"You know, I heard that in America there's this new app for hailing a private car. I think it's called Über. I'm not quite sure exactly how it works because it's so new – something about how you can get private car drivers instead of taxi drivers to drive you to your destination. I heard many taxi drivers went out of work," said his taxi-driver friend.

"Aiyoh!" said Teng with a worried look. "I've got a new flat and still paying it off. If Über ever comes to Singapore, then how? My earnings may be affected. And who knows, there may be other similar car hailing apps by local or regional companies too. I'm sure India will have its own app and China will have its own too. If they also come to Singapore, then die lah. I have a mortgage to pay.

"And what if the property market turns bad and the value of the flat kaput?"

Teng confided his concerns to Peter.

"Don't worry. You've already received a grant from the government. Consider yourself richer!" Peter reassured Teng.

"If this Über thing comes to Singapore, you work harder. You can. Anyway, I don't think Über will enter Singapore so soon. It will take a few more years. And you did the right thing, getting as high a floor as possible. When you resell, it will command a higher premium than a lower floor unit."

"Maybe I bought the wrong flat. It still troubles me that the railway line to JB is so near. I can hear the train every night. It's louder than I thought it would be. When people say sound travels up, it's true. Sometimes it wakes me up. It may be difficult to sell when I want to move," worried Teng.

"Don't worry. Anyway, you cannot sell in the next five years. Who knows what will happen in the future. Maybe there'll be no more railway line," Peter said, without realising how prophetic that statement would be.

Peace and Quiet

One day, Teng received repeated missed calls from Peter. But he couldn't pick up as he was driving a passenger.

Immediately after the passenger alighted, the call came again.

"What's the matter? You strike lottery ah?" joked Teng as he heard Peter's excited voice.

"Have you read today's papers? You are going to *fatt* (meaning 'prosper')!" Peter exclaimed.

"What are you talking about?"

"Malaysia and Singapore *gahmen* (Singlish expression for 'government') just announced that they are stopping the railway operations."

"Huh? What? Are you serious?"

"Yes, yes. It's all in the papers."

The governments of Malaysia and Singapore had reached a landmark agreement in May 2010 to end the nearly 80-year-old KTM (Keretapi Tanah Melayu) railway connecting Singapore and the Malay peninsula.

From 1 July 2011, KTM trains would stop passing through housing estates across the island. The land plots at Tanjong Pagar, Kranji, Bukit Timah, and Woodlands and 40-kilometre of rail tracks were to be returned to the Singapore government. In return, the Singapore government would allocate four parcels of land at Marina South and two parcels of land at Ophir-Rochor to a joint-venture firm, M+S Private Limited, set up by the two countries to develop the lands.

The Tanjong Pagar Railway Station located in the downtown area of Singapore, which also housed immigration and checkpoint facilities, would move to the new Woodlands Train Checkpoint near Singapore's end of the Johor–Singapore Causeway.

The cessation of railway operations would permanently remove the vibration and noise of passing trains that had affected residents living near the railway tracks and stations.

The cessation of railway operations would permanently remove the vibration and noise of passing trains that had affected residents living near the railway tracks and stations.

Teng couldn't believe the good news and looked forward to quiet nights in his neighbourhood. But such thoughts of peaceful slumber were interrupted by his more pragmatic friend.

"This means the prices of HDB flats in Woodlands will go up. You are rich."

He hadn't thought of that. But indeed, that was music to his ears.

Teng was smiling from ear to ear for the rest of the day. He couldn't wait to get home to see the look on Siew Ling's face when he broke the good news to her.

He invited Peter to his home for dinner that evening to strategise on what he should do with his flat.

History of KTM Railway

KTM Railway is a Malaysia state-owned firm that operated the railway services between Malaysia and Singapore since 1923. Both countries were then under British rule. The British colonial administrator gave the rights to use approximately 200 hectares of land in Singapore to KTM to operate train services. The tracks and lands were leased to KTM under two tenures — one for 999 years and the other in perpetuity; and were to be returned to the Singapore government if they were no longer used for their intended purposes.

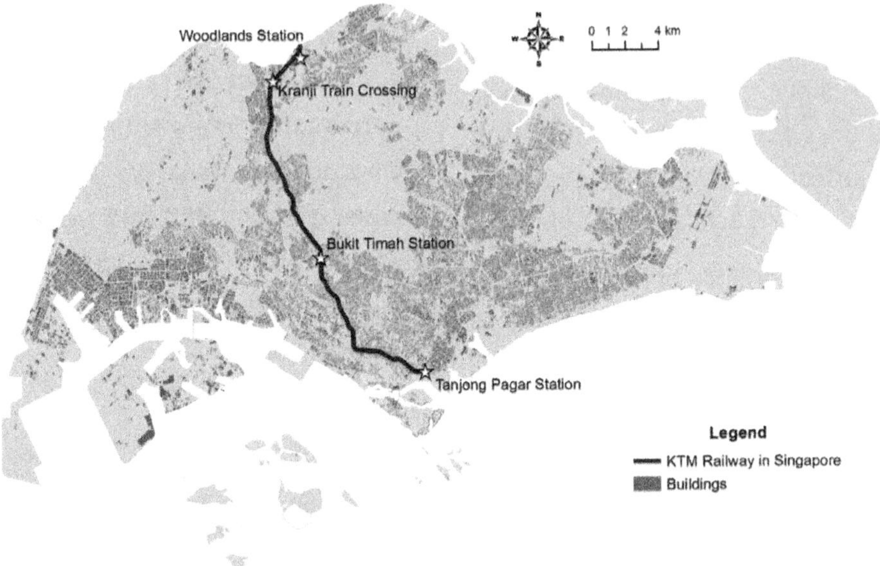

After the opening of the Johor–Singapore Causeway in 1923, the KTM train services were extended to JB to the north and in 1932, extended south to Tanjang Pagar, which also served as the embarkation and disembarkation point for KTM trains in Singapore.

While both governments had attempted to amend the KTM land rights, the agreements had been on and off; first between Singapore's then Prime Minister, the late Mr Lee Kuan Yew, and then Malaysian Finance Minister, Mr Tun Daim Zainuddin in 1990, and later with then Malaysian Prime Minister Dr Mahathir Mohamad in 1998, only to be aborted in 2002.

But on 28 June 2011, Mr Lee Hsien Loong, Prime Minister of Singapore, and Mr Najib Razak, Prime Minister of Malaysia, broke the two-decade impasse by sealing a landmark land-swop agreement, and signed the new land-swop deal.

Woodlands Home

Teng and Siew Ling had been living in their Woodlands flat for about two years. They could only sell the flat in another three years or so after satisfying the minimum occupation period of five years imposed by HDB.

Teng hoped this was the break he needed to have a better life for himself and Siew Ling.

On his way home, he stopped to get some roast duck and soya braised hard boiled eggs. These were Siew Ling's favourites.

"Wow! Today's so special ah," Siew Ling said with a smile as she unpacked the food for dinner. "You did something wrong is it?" she teased.

"Aiyah! No lah. Can't I give you a treat?" replied Teng, trying hard to suppress his joy. "Oh, Peter's joining us for dinner."

Siew Ling was puzzled. "Strange that Peter would just drop by on such short notice," thought Siew Ling. "These two must be up to no good."

Peter arrived bringing the newspapers with him.

With his big booming voice, he bellowed "*Fatt* ah! The God of Prosperity is smiling down at you," as he smacked Teng's back with the newspapers.

"What's going on?" asked Siew Ling curiously.

"Wait wait wait. Shh . . . Wait till we sit down for dinner. Then we talk," interjected Teng before Peter could answer.

Once dinner started, Peter chatted excitedly.

"Did you read today's papers? The Malaysian and Singapore *gahmen* have decided no more railway line. The details were announced today.

"We won't have the railway anymore. The KTM trains will stop passing through housing estates.

"That means, you lucky fella, you can enjoy peace and quiet without the trains rumbling across your backyard."

"Wow! Good ah. Now we can sleep properly. No need to explain to guests who come and wonder what that sound is," remarked a relieved

Siew Ling who was simplistically more concerned about her sleep and explaining the noise to guests than about the financial implications.

"That's what first came to my mind too," chimed in Teng.

"Aiyah! You two missed the point," cried an exasperated Peter, who perhaps because of his real estate background, was more pecuniarily savvy.

"No train means no noise. No noise means more money. I tell you. The value of your flat will sure go up."

Siew Ling and Teng looked at each other. There was a twinkle in their eyes. The dinner was good, indeed.

To celebrate the good news, they decided to engage in their favourite pastime and went to watch a late-night movie — *Iron Man 2* — which everyone had been raving about. It was like good times when they were dating.

Six Months Later

Peter came again. Like the previous time, there was a ring of excitement in his voice.

"What did I tell you? Six months ago, I said your property price will surely go up. I went to search my company's library and found this research by a group of professors.

"Is your flat within 400 metres from the railway line?"

"Hmm . . . I think so. We can see it from our bedroom and can walk there," replied Teng.

"And you can sell in a couple of years' time?" asked Peter.

"Yes, about there," Teng responded.

"Wonderful! You're in for a treat," Peter smiled smugly at himself for reading the property market so well.

"These NUS profs wanted to find whether the removal of the train noise will affect housing values. They studied the transactions of 221,000 non-landed private houses located within a five-kilometre boundary from the KTM railway lines. Of these, almost 9,900 were located within the KTM noise zone and the remaining 211,200 were outside. 'Noise zone' means within 400 metres of the railway line.

"They also measured the distance between the homes to the closest MRT station, to schools, to the CBD and to bus stations to see how these may influence property prices."

Both Teng and Siew Ling eagerly waited for Peter to deliver the good news to them.

"Your house is a three-room HDB flat. The profs studied condos, apartments and executive condos. But never mind. I think we can *agak agak* (meaning 'approximate') their findings to HDB flats.

"The profs also categorised the properties under 'new sale', 'subsale' and 'resale'. New sale units are units sold by the developer. Subsale units are sold by individual owners before the property is completed. And resale units are completed units sold by individual owners in the secondary market.

"Resale transactions within the KTM noise zone made up 62 percent of the total transactions. So don't play play because yours will be a resale when you sell it.

"They found that houses within 400 metres from the railway line were affected by the noise. Those living further beyond the distance were not affected. So I hope your flat is within 400 metres. If it is, you will be laughing your way to the bank.

"The profs did a 'before-and-after' study of how property prices changed.

"When it was first announced in May that there will be a KTM land-swop agreement, they found some strong 'anticipative effects' on the housing price increases."

"Huh? Why is Peter talking like that?" Teng wondered, "He sounds like the professor in the taxi who studied taxi drivers' behaviour."

[A]fter the announcement of the land swop but before the actual removal of the railway lines, ... these houses were already reselling at a higher price. People were pricing these houses higher in anticipation of the removal of the railway lines.

Peter elaborated, "What this means is that after the announcement of the land swop but before the actual removal of the railway lines, the profs found these houses were already reselling at a higher price. People were pricing these houses higher in anticipation of the removal of the railway lines.

"These house prices increased by between 2 to 3.3 percent. And this is based only on the announcement — the railway lines have not been removed yet.

"That's for the resale property. Even better is the new housing. Prices for new housing went up by 8.2 to 12.2 percent after the announcement. These developers are capitalising on the announcement. They are making more money from the sale of new and uncompleted houses compared to houses sold by owners in the resale market, just based on the announcement.

"Whether the prices will go up further, I don't know. But the profs did say they are continuing to study the effects after the railway lines have been removed. I will keep an eye out on this and update you."

His friends nodded in appreciation. They couldn't believe what they were hearing. Although the study was on private property, they quietly hoped the same good fortune would smile on their modest HDB flat.

"So, I tell you, if the same happens to your flat, *lei mo tuin tuin fatt tat* (meaning 'you prosper without having to do anything')," Peter broke out in Cantonese in the midst of excitement. "You have suddenly prospered not from your own doing. When you are ready to sell your flat, it's very likely that its price will go up just like the private properties."

Teng and Siew Ling were excited.

"I wonder whether such 'anticipative effects' also occur for other announcements," thought Teng.

"If a choice school were to be relocated, would the announcement of its relocation immediately reduce prices of houses near the original location and raise prices of properties in close proximity to the new location even before the school moves?

"Would an announcement of where new MRT stations will be enhance prices of properties in the proximity of these stations even before the stations are constructed?

"How about if it's a hospital? Some people like to live near a hospital especially when they have elderly family members. Yet, there are those who don't like it, because it reminds them of sickness and death – something ominous. Would an announcement of where a hospital will be affect property prices in the vicinity?"

Teng gathered his thought and said, "I think it would be interesting to study what type of new construction – school, MRT station, hospital or even shopping centre – will raise property prices. Don't you think so, Peter?"

Peter shrugged and gave him a nudge, "Whatever. Just don't forget to call me to be your agent when you are selling."

Teng gave him a thumbs-up.

WANT TO KNOW MORE?

This chapter is based on Diao Mi, Qin Yu and Sing Tien Foo, "Negative Externalities of Rail Noise and Housing Values: Evidence from the Cessation of Railway Operations in Singapore," *Real Estate Economics*, Vol. 44 (4), (2016), pp. 878–917.

CHAPTER 4

To Johor, to Johor, to Buy That Nice Dress

Peter's news of the potential increase in their house value brought cheer to Siew Ling's already pleasant disposition. Living in Woodlands initially appeared daunting. It seemed isolated from the rest of Singapore, being located right at the north, and a stone's throw away from neighbouring Malaysia. Many would describe Woodlands as *ulu* (meaning 'remote').

But living in Woodlands had its advantages. Siew Ling liked working at Good Fit at Woodlands Point. Though the shopping mall situated in a less densely populated suburban neighbourhood was somewhat small, Siew Ling found it appealing in a folksy kind of way. It reminded her of her growing-up years in Geylang where the shopkeepers knew their customers, and sometimes even called them by their name. Woodlands Point had that bit of the neighbourly *gotong royong* (meaning 'looking out for each other') atmosphere — a welcomed change from the sleek but sterile feel of high-end shopping malls in the city.

Siew Ling enjoyed shopping. Ever since she was four or maybe five years old, she had been interested in fashion. She noticed what others were wearing and how their dressing could be improved with a little less of something or a little bit more of another, or how the skirt length could be shortened for just that little bit of pizzazz.

That fashion interest had readily spurred her enthusiasm in other consumer products. After all, how many clothes can a girl buy? The fashionista had become a marketing maven. She knew the prices of various products, which retailer was going to have an upcoming sale, and whether a promotion was worth buying. From cosmetics to cooking oil, dresses to detergents, shoes to shampoo, Siew Ling had it all at her finger tips. She was a walking Google for shopping!

Shopping across the Border

Her shopping interest was further fanned by the proximity of her Woodlands flat to Johor. A direct four-kilometre journey by bus from her place to Johor beat the hour-long bus-cum-train ride to go to Orchard Road hands down.

But Siew Ling admitted that there was the slight hassle of alighting and boarding the bus at the checkpoint for the mandatory customs check. She had to be careful not to lose her passport amidst the throng of Singaporeans. That would be problematic.

Besides accessibility and transport convenience, there was that idea of attractive savings from shopping in Johor rather than in Singapore.

Once tagged as a shopper's paradise to attract tourists, Singapore became an expensive place to shop due to rising real estate prices and the introduction of the then 3 percent GST (Goods and Services Tax) in 1994.

Higher taxes are not necessarily a bad thing. At times, governments act for the good of the nation by imposing higher taxes on 'sin' and

Higher taxes are not necessarily a bad thing. At times, governments act for the good of the nation by imposing higher taxes on 'sin' and 'luxury' goods to discourage the consumption of these items.

'luxury' goods to discourage the consumption of these items. For example, Singapore taxes tobacco, alcohol and luxury cars at higher marginal tax rates.

With GST at 7 percent since 2007 and unlikely to decline, Siew Ling had been more careful with how she spent, especially since she and Teng intended to start a family and upgrade to a more centrally located residence eventually.

She could easily save 7 percent when she shopped in Malaysia, as the Malaysian government had yet to impose GST. Moreover, the exchange rate then favoured Singapore. Every $1 was about 2.4 Malaysian ringgit. With most products not adjusting completely to the exchange rate difference, Siew Ling, like many Singaporeans, was benefitting even more just by shopping across the border.

Pre-Johor Shopping

When Siew Ling first moved to Woodlands and was not familiar with the shopping jaunt in Johor, her sales colleague, Jothi, had told her, "The prices in JB are so much cheaper. Every Saturday morning, my husband will drive us to JB. We buy a lot of our groceries and household items there. As long as these are not branded, we can easily save 20 to 30 percent. That's a lot of money."

"Wow! That means for every four weeks of groceries, I can save one week's worth of shopping," said Siew Ling making quick mental calculations, honed by her many years of price comparisons while shopping.

"And after our shopping, we'll have a delicious and cheap *makan*," recounted Jothi.

"My children enjoy themselves and as a family, we take it as an outing – like going overseas. And because it's so cheap, we don't feel guilty about spending."

"No wonder I see my neighbour going out every Saturday and coming back with bags full of groceries from this place called Jusco. And I was wondering where Jusco is. I couldn't find it in Woodlands Point," Siew Ling said as she seemed delighted to have finally solved a mystery.

"Yes, that's a popular supermarket. Many Singaporeans go there for grocery shopping. Our local shops, especially those near the border, are suffering. The other day, the uncle from the convenience store complained that his business is so poor that he may have to close down. He told me his sales for snacks, detergent and soft drinks are so bad because Singaporeans buy them in JB. Who can blame them? After all, the Coke in Singapore is the same as the Coke in JB, right? But cheaper," added Jothi.

"Is it safe to shop in JB?" asked Siew Ling. "I hear all these horror stories of robberies."

"Wherever you go, you must use your common sense, right? Don't go to quiet lanes. Always shop where there are many people around," advised her friend.

Because I buy in JB, I don't have to use my card to buy the same things in Singapore and pay more! In fact, I find my credit card bill has gone down by about one-third.

"I tell you. It's worth shopping in JB, especially for Singaporeans living in Woodlands. After I started shopping there, I find my credit card expenses go down. Because I buy in JB, I don't have to use my card to buy the same things in Singapore and pay more! In fact, I find my credit card bill has gone down by about one-third. That's quite substantial, isn't it?" her friend added.

"Hmm . . . I wonder whether her credit card bill is less because she substituted what could have been credit card purchases in Singapore with cash in Malaysia," Siew Ling thought.

"So you pay your JB purchases with cash?" enquired Siew Ling.

"No, I still use my credit card in JB. Instead of buying the dress or groceries here, I use my card to buy the same or similar items in JB. The shampoo in Singapore is the same as the shampoo in Malaysia. So what for I buy in Singapore when it is more expensive?

"I also use my card to pay for lunch at JB instead of coming back to eat. My children enjoy such outings.

"I don't think I use more cash. It's my credit card expenses that I save on. All in, I'd say I save about one-third of my regular credit card expenses. Let me do a quick calculation," her friend went through a tiny booklet where she had neatly kept her expenses over the months.

A piece of paper slipped out as Jothi was ruffling through the pages. It showed what looked like graphs. Siew Ling picked it and handed it to Jothi.

"Thanks, Siew Ling. Hey, you might be interested in this. My husband got this from a talk he attended. It shows how much Singaporeans were spending on their credit cards every month on supermarket shopping and dining in Johor depending on whether they live close to or far from the Woodlands border. He gave it to me as he knows I love shopping," Jothi said as she showed her the piece of paper.

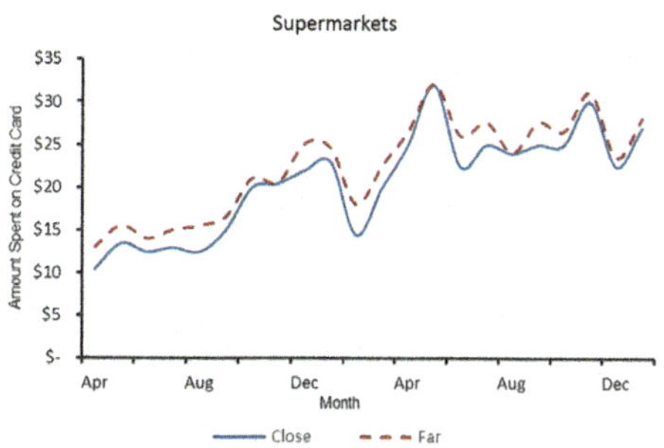

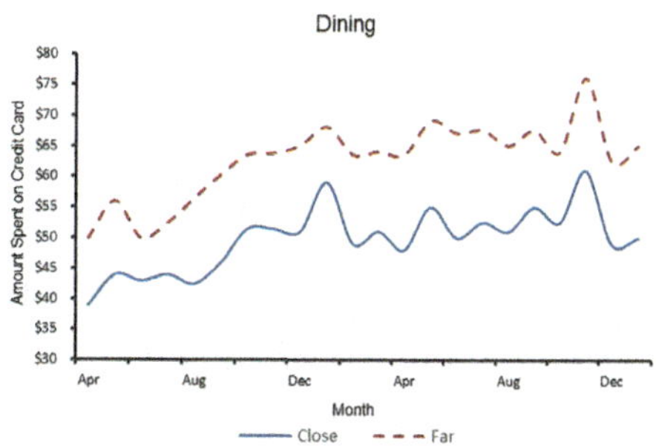

"You see the blue solid line? That's us — people who live near the Johor border and are more likely to shop in Johor. The red dashed line is for Singaporeans who live far from the border and are less likely to shop in JB. You see the blue line is always lower than the red line. This means we spend less on our total credit card bills for grocery shopping, and especially so for eating. Why? Because of JB lah."

Siew Ling looked in amazement as her colleague explained.

Then Jothi exclaimed as she found her expenditure pages, "Wow! I didn't realise that I saved so much. Yeah! Double confirm. I save one-third on my credit card bills without spending more on my debit card or using more cash.

I spend about a quarter less on dining because JB dining is cheap.... On entertainment, I spend about close to a fifth less.... My supermarket expenses for household products are about 15 percent less. For clothes, ... I save about 10 percent.

"Let me see my dining bills . . . I spend about a quarter less on dining because JB dining is cheap, and importantly, the food is yummy delicious! On entertainment, I spend about close to a fifth less — that's like 18 percent less. My supermarket expenses for household products are about 15 percent less. For clothes, my favourite, I save about 10 percent.

"The savings look a lot, but these are for products that don't matter where you buy, like groceries and dining — they are the same in Singapore and Malaysia. In fact, a lot of people say dining in Malaysia is better because the food there is a lot tastier than in Singapore.

"I think if I were living far from JB, say Bedok, I don't think my credit card spending will go down because it's unlikely I will be shopping in JB as often as I do now," observed Jothi.

"How about seeing doctor? You go there or not? Or how about your children's tuition?" asked Siew Ling.

"No lah. How can? Where got people sick in Singapore and travel to JB to see doctor? If you were sick, you go to the nearest doctor, not all the way to JB," Jothi looked incredulous at Siew Ling for asking such a question. "The savings are only for supermarket shopping, dining, buying clothes, entertainment and retail.

"Even more amazing is my cousin," she continued. "She shifted from east of Singapore, near Tampines, to Woodlands a year ago and started shopping in JB. She found her credit card bill went down by nearly half! Half, ok? That's huge savings.

"Her husband who is a chain smoker benefits most from cheaper shopping in JB. Items that have higher taxes like cigarettes are much cheaper in Malaysia. So he hardly buys cigarettes in Singapore except on the occasions he runs out of cigarettes. Then he has no choice but to buy in Singapore. Even so, he would buy the less expensive ones due to additional GST charges. Otherwise, he would simply buy from JB."

Then Jothi recounted the reverse scenario of a friend of hers.

"My friend who used to live in Woodlands but moved to Kembangan to be near her parents was complaining to me the other day. Now she doesn't go to JB to shop because it's just too far away. She misses her JB shopping.

"She said shopping in Singapore is so expensive. She tried to save. But still, in the end, her credit card expenses still go up. Even after trying very hard to be frugal, I think she said her credit card bill is something like 10 percent higher."

"Oh dear," thought Siew Ling. "I'd better remember that should we decide to move out of Woodlands."

"And Siew Ling, you are lucky you live near the Woodlands border, not the Tuas border. You know we can go to Johor from Woodlands or Tuas, right? My friend who lives at Tuas complained that there are hardly any shopping amenities at the border. So she still has to buy in Singapore. The other day, we were comparing how much we spend on our credit cards. I'm happy to say that I spend almost 10 percent less than she does."

"But maybe you spend less on your credit card and withdraw more cash? If so, it's the same thing in the end, right?" asked Siew Ling.

"Aiyah! As I've already told you, I withdraw the same amount of cash every month. It's on my credit card that I save. Why are you so sceptical?" replied her colleague.

"Anyway, with all these savings, my family will be going to Sentosa this weekend for a staycation. So fun!"

Shopping in JB and in Europe

After that conversation with Jothi, Siew Ling wondered whether her friend Shelley also had the same idea of shopping outside Singapore, especially for big-ticket items, to save on GST. She saw some similarities between shopping in JB and shopping in Europe — both concern shopping outside the Singapore border.

Shelley — tall, lithe and ever so poised — had been flying with Singapore Airlines for three years. Well-travelled and with an eye for all things classy, Shelley observed many brand name fashion merchandise to be cheaper in Europe than in Singapore. She had shared this observation with Siew Ling on several occasions.

"Last month when I was in Paris, I went to the Louis Vuitton store at Champs-Elysées. You won't believe it. It was so cheap. I was like . . . aahhh. And at the Hermès store, the line was so long. There were so many mainland Chinese tourists going there to buy Hermès and they even had good-looking Mandarin-speaking French salesmen serving them. Why? Because the Chinese are the big spenders! Likewise in Frankfurt, the Longchamp bags were not only cheaper than in Singapore, there was more variety, and the stores had the latest designs too. Mind you, they were all genuine items, not counterfeits," Shelley exclaimed excitedly.

"You know I'm not a spendthrift. But the prices are quite unbelievable – much cheaper than in Singapore! When I claimed for tax refund at the airport, it was like hitting another jackpot."

"So you bought a lot?" asked Siew Ling.

"No. I could only afford one. I bought an LV bag. But my colleagues who have been flying for years buy these bags on a regular basis. They bring them back and sell to *tai tais* (meaning 'wealthy women') and make money. Sometimes, these *tai tais* give them specific items to buy. It's like placing an order. Then my colleagues will buy those particular items," added Shelley.

"I wonder why it's cheaper to purchase them there than in Singapore. And in Europe on top of that. I can understand things being cheaper in JB, but in Europe? Paris? I would think their cost of living is higher," remarked Siew Ling.

"Well, I think for one, most items are cheaper in their home country than in a foreign country. Take MCM bags. The same MCM bag is cheaper in Seoul than in Singapore. There's no transportation costs to consider. Moreover, there's no import tax too. Second, is the tax savings. As a tourist, I save on sales tax in that country. And I also avoid sales tax in Singapore as I didn't buy it here. So no import tax, no foreign tax and no local tax. And that can be a hefty amount for high-end items," rationalised Shelley.

For this reason, Shelley had reduced her shopping expenditure in Singapore, even during the Great Singapore Sale. Siew Ling thought this was similar to what was happening in China, where high import taxes on luxury items were creating an outflow of funds due to Chinese nationals buying these merchandise in droves during their travels. Could this also be happening in Singapore with Singaporeans purchasing household items in JB because of the GST differential? Or in the instances of Singaporean tourists buying brand name fashion merchandise overseas?

And now with online shopping, which offered her variety and convenience, Siew Ling had less reason to shop in brick-and-mortar stores. Purchases of items not available in Singapore could be made with just a few clicks, and the ordered goods would be shipped to her doorstep for free, arriving in a matter of days. Siew Ling wondered how much Singaporeans' expenditures on online purchases were. She knew Amazon was gaining popularity among Singaporeans. "Are there any particular product types that do better online than others?" she wanted to know.

Maybe she could shop online instead of going to JB. But that would defeat the whole idea of shopping, which was to touch and try the items while soaking in the shopping spirit. "Anyway, shopping in malls is also a form of exercise," Siew Ling told herself. "Online shopping only exercises your fingers."

Less Expensive Shopping

Ever since Jothi advised Siew Ling to shop in JB, she and Teng had been doing their household purchases in JB as much as possible. True enough, they had been spending some one-third less on their credit card bills for the same items they would have bought in Singapore.

Teng was particularly pleased. He had been eyeing some brand name clothes in Singapore and was happy to find these items cheaper in JB. So he stocked up on them to wear when going out with his friends.

He wanted his friends to admire his fashion sense. And he lavished at the "oohs" and "ahhs" he got when he whipped out his Pierre Cardin leather wallet, bought at a much cheaper price in JB.

As a sales person, Siew Ling had to work on most weekends. But during her off days, she would take the bus into JB. That suited her just fine as the traffic to JB was less heavy on weekdays.

Being a savvy shopper like many Singaporeans, Siew Ling learnt to stretch her money.

As there's only so many shopping bags that she and Teng could carry, Siew Ling realised she ought to be more strategic — shop more for high-ticket items in JB while buying low-ticket items in Singapore. This made sense to her, as savings on more expensive products were likely to be more substantial than savings on cheaper items.

One day, while sitting in the bus on the way to Johor, she thought, "Our GST is actually encouraging Singaporeans like me to cross the border to shop in Malaysia. This will hurt local businesses, especially those small neighbourhood shops that Jothi had talked about. Worse still, the Singapore government will collect less GST revenue because we are shopping in Malaysia.

"Maybe the government should consider lowering GST so that Singaporeans will not be encouraged to shop in Johor. But I know that won't happen. Maybe the authorities should consider increasing income tax rate instead. Oh no! But that will affect Teng and me."

"Aiyah! Why am I thinking so much? I save money can already," said Siew Ling, resignedly to herself.

Siew Ling continued to be chirpy as she reached the Woodlands checkpoint. The thought of a higher value for her Woodlands flat coupled with the savings she made from shopping in Johor made her a happy shopper indeed.

WANT TO KNOW MORE?

This chapter is based on Sumit Agarwal, Souphala Chomsisengphet, Ho Teck-Hua and Qian Wenlan, "Tax Differential and Cross-Border Shopping: Evidence from Singapore," (1 March 2017). Available at SSRN: https://ssrn.com/abstract=2262070 or http://dx.doi.org/10.2139/ssrn.2262070; and Sumit Agarwal and Qian Wenlan, "What Shopping in Malaysia Means for Us," *Asian Business News*, (23 December 2016). http://www.business-support-network.org/asiabiz/author/sumit-agarwal-and-qian-wenlan/

CHAPTER 5

Gentlemen, Start Your Engines

The good news continued for Teng and Siew Ling. It seemed that since the announcement about the Woodlands train station last year, life was looking up for them.

In a surprise announcement as part of the February budget speech, the government announced that Singaporeans aged over 21 years old would be receiving a one-time payout ranging from $600 to $800 depending on their income and annual home value in what was called the Growth Dividend Programme (GDP).

In a surprise announcement as part of the February budget speech, the government announced that Singaporeans aged over 21 years old would be receiving a one-time payout ranging from $600 to $800 ... in what was called the Growth Dividend Programme (GDP).

The GDP was unanticipated. Teng could not recall his friends or anyone for that matter talking about it. There had also been no discussion of it in the media during the six months leading up to the Budget announcement.

"Whoo hoo!" Teng cheered with glee when he heard the news. It was a pleasant surprise, as past budget speeches had mostly focused on selected issues such as corporate taxes or conservancy charges. But this announcement affected and, most importantly, benefitted all adult Singaporeans.

"I think election is coming," remarked Peter, the cynical one. "Otherwise, why would the *gahmen* give us this free money? Our *gahmen* is like this – giving freebies when election is coming. After that, taxes go up."

"Aiyah! Why are you so like that? Got free money also complain," responded Muthu. Muthu had been struggling to make ends meet. Work had been erratic for him and any handout was good news.

"Come on. It's good news – whether it is to make the ground sweet for the coming election or not, why complain?" reasoned Teng.

Spending Ahead

Within a week of the announcement in February, the media was abuzz, discussing the unanticipated nature of the programme.

Many people were discussing what they'd do with the money.

"Teng, my friend. I usually don't ask people this, but can you lend me some money?" asked Muthu, quite sheepishly.

"You know, we've been having such a tough life with my work being off and on . . . and Priya has been working so hard to help keep us afloat, and she still hurries home to cook after work – I want to bring her and the three boys out for dinner, to give her a break.

"But I don't have money now. The GDP money will come only in April. I just need an advance now. I will pay you back when I receive the GDP."

"How much do you need?" asked Teng.

"$200?" asked a hopeful Muthu. "I'll use some for the dinner. I'm thinking of bringing them to Little India for *naan* and *tandoori*. Something better than *thosai* and *idli*. I also need to buy new school uniforms and shoes for my boys."

Even Peter was saying he would be going for a holiday.

"I saw the travel fair being advertised the other day. Looks like there are several good deals. My wife and I were originally thinking of just going to Malacca for a short holiday. But now with the GDP – the timing is so *choon* (meaning 'timely or accurate') – we decided to upgrade. Instead of going to Malacca, we'll go to Bangkok. So I'm going to quickly sign up for the trip. Otherwise, if I wait till I get my GDP money, the promotion will be over.

"And I'll pay using my credit card. That way, I get points too!" laughed Peter.

No one knew exactly how much each would get. But $600 was guaranteed. There was an air of excitement. Teng was hoping he and Siew Ling would get the upper bound.

"How should we use the money?" asked Siew Ling.

Although the Lunar New Year was just over and she still had new clothes she had purchased just for that festivity, she had also been eyeing other dresses that she had held back from buying. There was one in particular – a sleeveless hot pink dress, much like the one worn by Kim So-yeon in the Korean drama, *Prosecutor Princess*. Siew Ling, a fan of Korean dramas, had also followed the fashions touted in the series quite closely. She was hoping that Teng would let her freely spend the money.

"Hehehe," snickered Teng. "You want to buy something right?"

Siew Ling replied, "I know we should save the money. But we've been working so hard, and saving quite a bit by shopping in JB."

"I know what you mean," nodded Teng. "We'll have at least $1,200 between the two of us. That's a lot of money.

"And really, this money is a windfall. We weren't expecting it. It just fell on our lap," he added.

He recalled how Muthu had borrowed money from him to spend in anticipation of receiving the extra money. But of course, Muthu was in a different situation. He was not gainfully employed and barely had savings after spending on necessities.

But Peter who, among the three of them, was the most contented had also expressed that he would be spending even before receiving the cash.

It seemed like many were spending ahead, before the payout was given.

"Ok, lah. Just go get what you want to buy. It's the government's gift to us. Enjoy it while we can," Teng laughed. He was thinking of upgrading his mobile phone and getting a sleek watch. He still enjoyed showing off what he had to others.

"Yeah! I'd better quickly get the dress before someone else buys it," reasoned Siew Ling, even though she would not be receiving the money until two months later.

Spending More Than Given

In April, Teng and Siew Ling each received a letter informing them that their individual payout was $700 each, which totalled $1400. Not too bad for free money.

They had already spent about $240 on Siew Ling's dress and a pair of matching shoes, and a few nice shirts and pants for Teng. And they had made out a list of other things to buy in the coming months, including the watch and upgraded mobile phone, plus the increased spending during the Great Singapore Sale in June and July.

"I wonder whether other Singaporeans are like us, spending ahead before we got the money — and even after getting the money, continue spending instead of saving," Teng wondered aloud to Siew Ling.

"Well, if they do, then the GDP is quite good. The government gives people money, and the people return the money by spending. Good for the economy, right?" Siew Ling remarked with the mind of a savvy shopper.

"Huh? What do you mean?" asked Teng.

"I heard my manager say that the GDP can help to sti-mu-late the economy. That means make the economy better," replied Siew Ling.

"If people spend what the government has given to us, then that money goes to businesses who will then have more sales. With more sales, businesses can expand. Otherwise, if they don't have enough sales and they close shop, then there'll be unemployment. But with more business, the economy can grow," explained Siew Ling.

"Wow! You are a smart cookie, wifey," said a surprised Teng, impressed.

"No lah. I overheard my manager say this over the phone," responded Siew Ling. "He was telling his friend that he read a university research report that studied the financial transactions of more than 180,000 individuals.

[F]or every $1 GDP we receive, on average we spend about $0.80 more in the months after receiving the GDP money.

"The report found for every $1 GDP we receive, on average we spend about $0.80 more in the months after

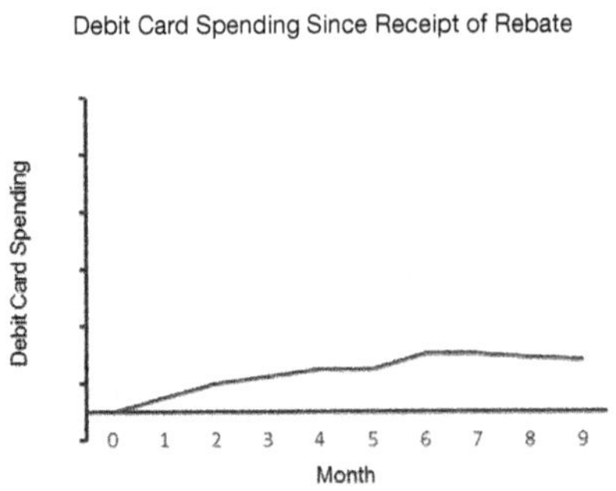

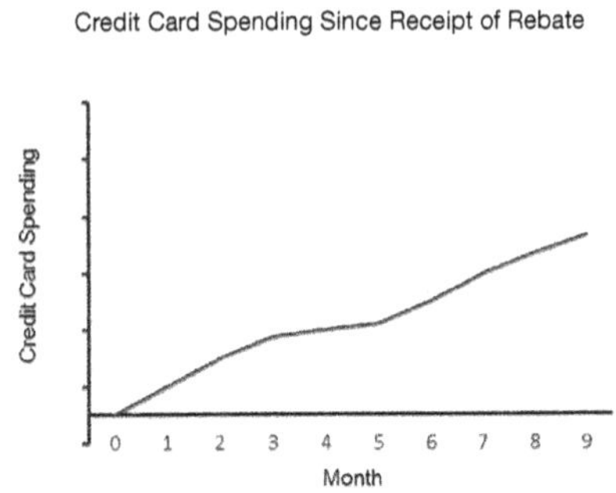

receiving the GDP money. Of course, we spend more at the beginning and less as time goes by.

About two-thirds of the increase in spending (or $0.53 per $1 received) is charged to credit cards, while one-third (or $0.26 per $1 received) is due to spending on debit cards.

"About two-thirds of the increase in spending (or $0.53 per $1 received) is charged to credit cards, while one-third (or $0.26 per $1 received) is due to spending on debit cards.

"I took a sneak peek at the report. My boss was holding it in his hands. There were two graphs — one on debit card spending and the other on credit card spending.

"In the months after receiving the growth dividends, spending went up but more so for credit card spending than debit card spending," said Siew Ling, explaining the graphs that she saw.

"But not everyone behaved the same way," she elaborated. "Low-income Singaporeans increased their spending more so than high-income Singaporeans. They would spend $0.20 per dollar

Low-income Singaporeans increased their spending more so than high-income Singaporeans. They would spend $0.20 per dollar received on their debit card and $0.61 per dollar received on their credit cards.

received on their debit card and $0.61 per dollar received on their credit cards. But richer Singaporeans did not spend much more leh. Maybe because they already spent a lot or already bought whatever they had to buy. Or maybe, the GDP amount was peanuts to them."

"Wow! I always thought money is money. I didn't think it would be different to the rich and poor," said Teng.

"Yeah. And not only that. How they spend their money also depends on age and whether you're Chinese or Indian," elaborated Siew Ling.

"I heard my manager say that while the young and old spent about $0.72 of every dollar received on their credit cards, older Singaporeans did not increase their debit card spending. But the young, who seem to haven't learn how to save, would spend $0.36 on their debit card for every $1 received. Maybe the young have a lot of things to buy.

"And the Chinese . . . Chinese Singaporeans spent a lot more on both types of cards while Indian Singaporeans tend to save the GDP."

"Ahh . . . That sounds exactly like us — low-income, young and Chinese. We are the ones who spend more," said Teng with a guilty look.

"My manager also said that it was interesting to note how we started to spend almost immediately after we heard the announcement, even though we had yet to receive the money," continued Siew Ling. "We spend $0.074 more per month for every $1 expected in the two months after the announcement, even before obtaining the payout.

[W]e started to spend almost immediately after we heard the announcement, even though we had yet to receive the money.

"So for example, if you were to receive $600, you would have spent about $44.40 more for each of the two months — March and April — even before receiving the money. And this spending was mainly on credit card, not debit card."

"Sounds like us, doesn't it?" said a concerned Teng. "We spend first before we got the money."

"Not only that, we also used our credit cards to spend the money that we had yet to receive," added Siew Ling. "And when we got the cash, we spent more on both our credit and debit cards.

"My manager also said that debit card spending went up mostly after we got the payout, while credit card spending just continued to be high. So it is the credit card that facilitated such spending amid this unexpected windfall.

"He also said that ATM (automatic teller machine) transactions did not change and that cash spending was not affected by GDP. So he told us that the shop will be installing credit card facilities soon to accept credit and debit card transactions. You know lah, the shop owner is so traditional and hasn't quite moved with the times. So this young manager recommended to the owner that we should have credit/debit card facilities. Otherwise, we'll lose out on this group of spenders should there be another surprise bonus."

"Eh . . . So we've been helping the Singapore economy when we go shopping," teased Teng.

"But jokes aside, our government is quite smart, don't you think? First, give us the growth dividend. It's like a freebie. But actually, since most of us spend almost all the money instead of saving it, we are helping the government stimulate the economy," Teng continued. "Do other countries do the same thing?"

"Well, I heard my manager say in America, they give tax rebates which you more or less expect every year. But the GDP was unexpected. I think because it was unexpected, one may say that the effects on spending are different," replied Siew Ling.

"Hmm . . . Anyway, I think we have spent all the $1,400 already, or maybe even more. So wifey, no more special propping up the Singapore economy through shopping," said Teng lovingly to his wife.

"Except during the Great Singapore Sale," said Siew Ling, having the last word.

WANT TO KNOW MORE?

This chapter is based on Sumit Agarwal and Qian Wenlan, "Consumption and Debt Response to Unanticipated Income Shocks: Evidence from a Natural Experiment in Singapore," *American Economic Review*, Vol. 104 (12), (2014), pp. 4205–4230; and Sumit Agarwal and Qian Wenlan, "Simulate and Stimulate," *The New Paper*, (15 April 2016). http://www.tnp.sg/news/views/simulate-and-stimulate

CHAPTER 6

Ladies, Ready, Get Set, Shop

Unlike other sales that are independently initiated by the retailer, the Great Singapore Sale (GSS) is a concerted government effort to get Singaporeans and tourists to shop by pushing retailers on a national scale to engage in price cuts.

[T]he Great Singapore Sale (GSS) is a concerted government effort to get Singaporeans and tourists to shop by pushing retailers on a national scale to engage in price cuts.

Started in 1994, the sale has since been held from June to July every year. Its regularity makes it possible for shoppers like Siew Ling to know how to adjust their spending accordingly. She would hold off the less urgent purchases until the start of the GSS to make her money work harder.

While Teng had always obliged Siew Ling, bringing her for her Orchard Road shopping in his taxi, she didn't want to rely on him all the time.

After all, ferrying her in his taxi incurred an opportunity cost: he wouldn't be able to pick up a paying passenger, which meant revenue lost. With plans to sell off their Woodlands flat after the discontinuation of the train service and relocate to a more central location, they needed to conserve whenever they could.

Its regularity makes it possible for shoppers ... to know how to adjust their spending accordingly.

"Don't worry," said Teng. "I can bring you to ION Orchard. From there, there's always people waiting for a taxi. I can easily pick up passengers. So my trip to downtown is not wasted."

Still, Siew Ling resisted.

ERP and Shopping

There was also the ERP system to contend with. Since 1998, all Singapore vehicles have been equipped with a car transponder called the In-vehicle Unit (IU) with preloaded cash card for electronic toll payment. Gantries are placed in areas known to face traffic congestion. The toll rate, with increments of 50 cents to $1, serves as a congestion tax to minimise traffic jams.

Siew Ling didn't want Teng to spend needlessly — it was not just the opportunity cost of driving her to town she was concerned about, but also the additional charges of paying the toll.

Even Teng had remarked before that he tried to avoid places where he had to pay the electronic toll.

"I don't mind paying because it's part of doing business. But if there were passengers in the taxi already, they have to pay. Sometimes, when we go past the gantry and the toll charge is shown on my taxi's IU, I can hear them grumbling quietly.

Siew Ling also felt the pinch. She remembered once when the toll charges were raised, she conscientiously tried to take public transport instead of relying on Teng.

She recalled discussing it with her shopping friends. There were about 10 of them.

"Hey, with the increase in ERP, do you still get your husband to drive you downtown or do you take public transport like the bus?" someone in the group had asked.

"If it's in the morning when I'm just starting my day, I'd switch to taking the public bus," said Rachael.

Bonnie nodded in agreement.

It appeared that two of her 10 friends had switched to public transport because of the ERP hike, but only for morning trips.

"If it's in the evening, and I'm kind of tired already, I don't take public transport. How about you Bonnie?" asked Rachael.

"I still take the bus, whether morning or evening. And I've been doing this for the last two months since switching," replied Bonnie.

Siew Ling felt that if she was going downtown, she should be taking the bus or the MRT sometimes too. The ERP hike may not make driving through the gantries justifiable. She'd rather use Teng's cab service in the evening, when she had finished her shopping and had lots of shopping bags to carry.

After all, she's been getting exhausted more easily of late. Sometimes, a little queasy too. Something inside her told her that they needed to save for an important impending expenditure. Call it woman's intuition. If her intuition was right, her GSS spending would have to be on things for something else other than herself or Teng.

GSS Shoppers

Siew Ling's intuition was spot on. The doctor confirmed that she was three months pregnant.

"Oh no! . . . I haven't worn that new dress yet and pretty soon, I won't be able to fit into it," thought Siew Ling regretfully, recalling the dress and the shoes she had bought with her growth dividend money.

Not that having a baby was bad news. They had always wanted one but had debated when to start. It was a dilemma between having a healthy baby when young or taking a risk of having a less-than-healthy child when older, but under a more financially comfortable position.

"I need to be more careful now with my money. I have to make sure that it is well spent," thought Siew Ling. "I'd better curb my spending before GSS so that I can make full use of the sale."

She found that all her shopping friends had done likewise. They knew there would be some good bargains to be had in June and had postponed their spending till GSS came.

They had met up one day at the end of June, midway through the GSS. Some had shopped at Takashimaya, others at Robinsons. With weary feet and bags full of purchases, Siew Ling and her friends were having drinks to quench their thirst after a whole day of intensive shopping.

Chatting animatedly about their purchases, the youngest of them, 22-year-old Maya, said, "I've been shopping almost non-stop since GSS started. For almost every day, I've been going to shopping centres in Orchard Road as well as in Jurong and Bedok for the best buys. Three weeks, non-stop. Marathon shopping!"

"Wow! You have so much energy. I shopped for only one week and got tired already. I didn't go anywhere during the second week. And then I started shopping again only last week," said Lay Gek, the oldest of them with three children.

"That's the difference between the young and the old," laughed Usha, their Indian shopping buddy. "The young just spend because it's on sale. It becomes a spree. I think it's because they are single. They have lots of money to spend on themselves, while the older ones pace themselves and are more careful. So, Lay Gek, what did you buy?"

The young just spend because it's on sale. It becomes a spree. I think it's because they are single. They have lots of money to spend on themselves, while the older ones pace themselves and are more careful.

"Clothes," said Lay Gek.

"Me too. Robinsons had such a fantastic sale. And since I'm a Robinsons member, I get another 5 percent additional savings on top of the hefty GSS discounts. I literally can shop till I drop," replied young Maya. "But it's not that I buy every time I go out. Sometimes I don't buy. But when I do buy, I definitely spend more."

"Yah, I agree. For the first week — it was crazy, man. I was spending left, right and centre. But after that, I was more disciplined," said the older Lay Gek.

"Aiyah, I wasn't disciplined at all. I just *qiong* (meaning 'do quickly without thinking'). I think I've been spending just as much from Week 1 to Week 4," cried Maya, the young shopper.

"Like what Usha said, that's because you're single. You can afford it. I've got three kids, you know. So I need to be more careful," said Lay Gek.

"I think I'm better than you Lay Gek. I only spend more, and even then not that much more, after the first week. I didn't rush in to buy immediately," said Usha, proud that she had been regulating her shopping expenses.

"Steady, girlfriend!" said Maya cheering Usha. "And I used my credit cards first. Then I can get points too. And after maxing out on my credit cards, I used my debit card."

All the ladies nodded in agreement. That was how they used their cards too. It's amazing how alike they were when carrying out their shopping.

"But I always wonder whether I should always try to use the same credit card for my purchases to get the points for redemption or have an assortment of cards and use them accordingly for the different benefits? If I spread my usage across cards depending on which card has what benefits, I won't be able to accumulate my frequent usage points for instance," Maya reflected, being the least experienced on credit card and shopping matters.

"I concentrate on using two cards only," replied Usha. "And these are the two cards that have the most benefits to me. That way, I get the benefits that I want and still accumulate points.

"And why two cards? Number 1, I can't keep track of all of them. Number 2, I'm scared I'll lose some of the cards or be exposed to fraudulent practices – and that will be big trouble. Number 3, if I don't spend enough on the third or fourth card, I'll be penalised with an annual registration fee which I'm not willing to pay."

"I'm just the reverse," said Lay Gek. "I have a deck of credit cards from various banks. I use my UOB Ladies cards for discounts when buying clothes, American Express to buy airline tickets because it has the Singapore Airlines affiliation, Maybank Family Card for discounted entertainment expenses like when I visit Universal Studios with my family, Citibank because it has the rewards system that credits to your account automatically, and POSB card for my grocery shopping," Lay Gek explained as she gave a laundry list of her cards issued by different banks. "Or wait, there's also the DBS card because I'm my husband's supplementary cardholder."

"Do you use credit card all the time?" asked Usha.

"All the time, even when buying gifts. Why should I use a debit card? It doesn't make sense. When you use a debit card, the money is deducted immediately from your bank account. For credit cards, you have like a month to pay, which frees up cash for other uses. My banker husband educated me on this," explained Lay Gek.

"I wish someone had advised me on this earlier, though I had read something about this in *The Sunday Times*," said Maya.

"How about you, Siew Ling? What did you buy?" asked Lay Gek.

"Uhh . . .," Siew Ling wasn't quite sure whether to share the good family news with her friends yet. "We have to be careful with how we spend. But we definitely have been spending more throughout this month to take advantage of the Great Singapore Sale.

"Especially for big-ticket durable products, we've been buying those first. If there's money left over, then we'll buy non-durables," replied Siew Ling.

"What do you mean 'durables'? Thought you've got all your furniture, TV, everything already," quizzed Maya.

Siew Ling was caught in a bind. She had inadvertently let the cat out of the bag. It seemed like she would have to tell her friends the good news after all.

"Teng and I bought a crib and cabinets. We are expecting our first baby," gushed Siew Ling.

"Congratulations!" her shopping friends chimed in unison.

"That's wise — buy big-ticket items first. Then spend the balance on consumables," nodded Lay Gek. "You are a savvy shopper!"

WANT TO KNOW MORE?

This chapter is based on Sumit Agarwal, Koo Kang Mo and Qian Wenlan,"Consumption Response to Temporary Price Shock: Evidence from Singapore's Annual Sale Event," (2013). Working Paper, National University of Singapore; Sumit Agarwal, Qian Wenlan and Koo Kang Mo, "Assessing the Impact of the Great Singapore Sale," *Think Business*, (22 June 2016); and Sumit Agarwal and Koo Kang Mo, "Impact of Electronic Road Pricing (ERP) Changes on Transport Modal Choice," *Regional Science and Urban Economics*, Vol. 60, (September 2016), pp. 1–11.

CHAPTER 7

Muthu, Don't Be Reckless

With a baby along the way, their three-room flat would soon not be big enough. Teng and Siew Ling were thinking of registering for a bigger flat — a four-roomer flat to accommodate the baby and Teng's parents. They would need his parents to help look after the baby. Having his parents move in would also allow Teng to keep an eye on them in their silver years.

His younger sister was already married with a child whom her in-laws were helping to look after. So she did not need Ma and Pa's help with childcare. His younger brother was living on his own.

His parents could rent their flat out for that extra pocket money and Teng wouldn't need to give them as much monthly allowance as he used to. It would be a win-win for all.

Of course, owning an HDB flat was still far from Teng's ideal dream home. Since young, he had fancied living in a condominium. He liked the idea of having a pool and gym. He would also be able to invite his friends over for a barbeque and have a good party at the function room. They would envy him.

But that was merely a dream. Taxi driving would not earn him the kind of money needed to buy a condo. At least Teng was realistic enough to know that that was a pipe dream – unless he could strike it big in the Singapore Sweep, a local lottery game with a handsome cash prize.

While there were new units available in new estates such as Sengkang, Teng preferred those in mature estates like Queenstown.

He was also thinking of the primary school that his unborn child would go to. He recalled the scouts' campfire he went to in his youth. There were the fancy cars waiting for the students attending that all-boys Methodist school. Teng liked the idea of having some form of religious grounding for young children. So he thought Fairfield Methodist School, a co-ed primary school, would be a good bet. If he wanted to enrol his child there, he would need to look for a flat in Dover.

But he also knew that Siew Ling liked visiting Nex, the mall in Serangoon. For whatever reason, her shopping trails more often than not, led her either to Orchard Road or to Nex. He could see her enjoying living in that neighbourhood.

However, he also needed to consider that if they were to buy a new HDB flat again, this would be their second application and they would not be entitled to the grant. In fact, they would have to pay a levy.

Also if they were to register for a new flat, they would probably have to wait for another three to four years before they could move in. In the meantime, perhaps they could make do with their current three-room flat even after factoring in the addition of their first child and his parents moving in. But the flat would be too small for their baby to walk or run in with Ma and Pa keeping a watchful eye.

Or should they buy a resale flat from the secondary market instead?

Teng got a headache thinking of the different options and paths that they could take.

He was counting on his real estate agent friend Peter to help him. Peter had given them the good news earlier that their flat could potentially enjoy an appreciation of about 3 percent with the cessation of the KTM rail services. They were relying on him to seek a potential buyer whom they could sell their Woodlands flat to, and to find a tenant for Ma and Pa's flat, or sell it if they wished to.

Unravelling

"Teng, I've some bad news," rang Peter one day. "Priya, Muthu's wife, called. She was crying. It seems Muthu is in really bad shape. He has so much debt. He can't pay."

"Hah? What happened? I lent him $200 the other time. He said he would pay me when he gets the GDP money. Though I never intended to chase him, because I know he doesn't have enough money – but I didn't know it is so bad," replied Teng.

Peter continued, "It seems he went into some kind of business and lost everything – the little that he had. You know how it is with Muthu. Last time in school, he was always the one who took risks. He's not scared, always thinking he can get rich the fast way.

"So he went into this business of getting people to invest in some properties in Latin America. I think this was what happened because Priya was quite hysterical. Apparently, he had a partner but either the partner played him out or the business did not take off. I'm not sure what really happened but in the end, all the money's gone."

"*Wah piang eh* (Singlish equivalent of 'holy moly'). He bankrupt ah?" asked the shocked Teng. The news shook Teng to the core. Muthu had been one of his buddies since primary school.

"I think so, because Priya said they haven't paid their mortgage and electricity bills for several months. HDB and Singapore Power have been hounding them. I think the $200 you lent him went into this business because Priya said she didn't know about it. The kids didn't get new uniforms or shoes and she still cooks every meal."

"My $200 doesn't matter. How about Muthu? How is he handling it?" Teng enquired, concerned.

"I don't know. I'm still finding out," said Peter.

"How come such things can happen? How did Muthu become like that?" Teng asked in disbelief. "He has three boys, you know. He needs to be more responsible."

Bankruptcy in Singapore

Declaring bankruptcy is associated with a negative social stigma, even though it is actually a legal process for those facing financial difficulties.

In Singapore, where traditional Asian values run deep, overgeneralised beliefs often mistakenly assume bankruptcy to be a consequence of or punishment for immoral behaviour or personal irresponsibility. As such, bankrupts not only feel terrible about declaring bankruptcy, but are also labelled as irresponsible spenders.

In Singapore, where traditional Asian values run deep, overgeneralised beliefs often mistakenly assume bankruptcy to be a consequence of or punishment for immoral behaviour or personal irresponsibility. As such, bankrupts not only feel terrible about declaring bankruptcy, but are also labelled as irresponsible spenders.

According to Singapore's bankruptcy law, assets belonging to a bankrupt — except for necessities that are needed to make a living – are seized. A bankrupt is also required to seek consent from creditors for a number of activities, including running a business, traveling overseas and even taking a taxi as the latter is considered a non-essential expense.

Profile of a Bankrupt

"Eh, I tell you . . . the conveyancing lawyer I usually work with for the properties I sell told me this," shared Peter. "He heard from his colleague, also a lawyer, that men are more likely to become bankrupt than women. Apparently, there was a study done on gender and bankruptcy in Singapore.

"The study wanted to find out whether there are gender differences in risk attitudes that may result in differential bankruptcy filings.

"It used two sources of data. The first data source has over 65,000 personal bankruptcy filings at the Supreme Court of Singapore. For each bankruptcy case, it recorded information relating to the debtor, the bank or creditor, and total bankruptcy amount.

"The bankruptcy cases they studied were related to credit cards. $10,000 was the cut-off used to separate credit card bankruptcy cases from other bankruptcy cases involving home mortgage and car loan delinquencies."

"Eh, Peter. How come your English so good now? You speak like those *jiak kan tan*," asked Teng, referring to Peter's proper English (*jiak kan tan* literally means 'eat potatoes', implying speaking in proper English like people who eat potatoes – Westerners).

"Aiyah! I want to be professional. I have to deal with expats coming to Singapore to work. They rent properties. And many also eventually become permanent residents and want to buy properties too. So my boss told me I have to brush up on my English. That's why I've been reading and practising," Peter explained.

"If only I'd done that in school! My exam results would have been better," Teng said with a tinge of regret.

"Anyway, back to what the lawyer said," Peter continued. "The researchers also distinguished repeated bankrupts involved in multiple bankruptcy events from first-time bankrupts involved in only single bankruptcy events. This is important because the risk attitude of recalcitrant debtors in repeated bankruptcy events may be different from those with only one bankruptcy record.

"The second data set contains information on gender, date of birth, ethnicity, marital status, public or private residence and postal code of more than 2 million individuals in Singapore.

"So the study is quite comprehensive."

"What did they find?" asked Teng.

"You guess? Do you think men or women are more likely to be bankrupted?"

"Men lah. We gamble, drink and smoke," Teng replied without hesitation.

"You're right. They found that for every four men who filed for personal bankruptcy, there is only one female bankrupt. And on top of that, women are less likely to encounter multiple bankruptcies than men. In fact, women are 36 percent less likely to encounter multiple bankruptcies than men. So my friend, we are more inclined to be bankrupt than our wives!"

[F]or every four men who filed for personal bankruptcy, there is only one female bankrupt.... [W]omen are less likely to encounter multiple bankruptcies than men.... [W]omen are 36 percent less likely to encounter multiple bankruptcies than men.

"*Alamak* (meaning 'oh gosh')! Our wives are better at handling money than us. We mustn't tell them that," joked Teng.

"Maybe women learn from their financial mistakes better than men. So they don't repeat getting into a bankruptcy again," suggested Peter.

"But why are they less likely to be bankrupt in the first place?" enquired a curious Teng.

"I asked my lawyer friend that question too," Peter replied. "He said his friend told him it's partly because of risk appetite. Men are more gungho — they dare to take risks. In the end, sometimes their risks are not justifiable. Somehow, men take less calculated risks than women. And this leads to more men becoming bankrupt. To put it another way, it means that women are likely to take less risk and behave less aggressively in personal financial management.

"Just like Muthu, lah. Remember how last time in school when we played football, he would just *qiong* and tackle the other side and hurt himself? I think Muthu likes to take risks.

"Even this business he went in — investing in real estate in Latin America. What does he know about property? How does he know if these properties actually exist? What if they were slums? I don't think I would do it. It's just too risky."

Teng nodded as he recollected the various risky moves that Muthu had made in school and as a working adult.

"And think of the numerous road accidents he has gotten himself into," Peter continued. "He's so accident prone. I think he zooms in and out on his motorbike quite recklessly. Remember when we visited him at Singapore General Hospital after he crashed his bike into the Porsche? I think Muthu thought he could outrace the car. He is quite a risk taker.

"Maybe that kind of reckless behaviour translated into him taking financial risks. He borrowed from several people to get into these quick-buck businesses that never materialised."

"So we better not play play when it comes to money," warned Teng.

"And you know what?" continued Peter. "Even the average bankruptcy amount differs between male and female bankrupts. Women bankrupt on a lesser amount. I think my lawyer friend said something like $222 less on average compared to male bankrupts.

"Worse still, my friend said that this man–woman difference for bankruptcy is more obvious among Chinese than Malay or Indian. Not only are there far more Chinese men filing for bankruptcy than Chinese women, these men are also more likely to file for multiple bankruptcies.

Not only are there far more Chinese men filing for bankruptcy than Chinese women, these men are also more likely to file for multiple bankruptcies.

"For Malays and Indians, the gap is smaller. What this means is that for the same number of male debtors, there are more Malay and Indian female debtors facing bankruptcy than Chinese female debtors."

"That's not comforting to hear," said Teng. "I wonder whether it also varies by dialect groups. You know what they say — Hokkiens are more aggressive and *pai kia* (Hokkien for 'naughty child'). Maybe Hokkiens take more risks and so land up with higher chances of being bankrupt. Did your lawyer friend say so?"

"No, he didn't mention that. I'll ask him later," replied Peter.

"But he did say that this gender gap persists and is even more pronounced among people living in HDB flats than those living in private housing. This means that men are more likely to be a bankrupt

[T]his gender gap persists and is even more pronounced among people living in HDB flats than those living in private housing. This means that men are more likely to be a bankrupt than women, but especially more so among those living in HDB flats than private residences.

than women, but especially more so among those living in HDB flats than private residences."

"Huh . . . that means us — because we are males, Chinese and HDB dwellers. This is triple tragedy," cried Teng in dismay. He reminded himself to tell his sister and brother this so that they do not go overboard with their expenses.

"And not only that, this gender gap widens with age. The older we get, the higher are our chances of going bankrupt and the lower are the chances of our wives getting bankrupt!" exclaimed Peter.

"That means we must involve our wives more in financial decision making, especially for big-ticket items. They seem to be more responsible with money," said an enlightened Teng. "But back to Muthu. What will happen to him?"

"I don't know. Things are still unfolding. He might go to jail. But for ourselves, we should be more careful and not take unnecessary risks especially when the economy is rocky."

WANT TO KNOW MORE?

Sumit Agarwal, He Jia, Sing Tien Foo and Zhang Jian, "Gender Gap in Personal Bankruptcy Risks: Empirical Evidence from Singapore," *Review of Finance* (forthcoming). Available at SSRN: https://ssrn.com/abstract=2340371 or http://dx.doi.org/10.2139/ssrn.2340371; and Sumit Agarwal, Sing Tien Foo and Zhang Jien, "Gender Gap in Bankrupt Risks: Its Meaning for Policy at Home, at Work," *The Business Times*, (6 December 2016). http://www.businesstimes.com.sg/opinion/gender-gap-in-bankruptcy-risks-its-meaning-for-policy-at-home-at-work

CHAPTER

Mind Your 4s and 8s

"Teng, our house is getting too small," complained Siew Ling, struggling to have her voice heard over Ethan's cries. Ethan was born a month ago, and had been exercising his lungs ever so often since.

Teng and Siew Ling had named their firstborn after Ethan Hunt, their favourite Mission Impossible secret agent character. They thought it was unique until they heard several other parents calling their son 'Ethan' too.

"He'll be walking in a year's time and I don't think we have enough space. We'd better move to a bigger place soon," said Siew Ling.

"Also, remember what Peter told us about how our flat is likely to have gone up in value because of the termination of the train services to Malaysia? I think it's about time to consider upgrading."

They had been toying with the idea of registering for a new flat. But Teng had been slow in finding out more from HDB and getting things moving.

As this would be their second application for a new flat, they would not be entitled to receive a grant. That made him to have second thoughts. Maybe, it would be easier to have Peter find them a resale flat.

Teng knew Siew Ling liked the Serangoon area because of its proximity to Nex, one of her favourite suburban shopping malls. Personally, he preferred the Queenstown neighbourhood. So, there were Serangoon and Queenstown areas to look at. A flat in Dover could also be a plausible choice due to its proximity to his preferred primary school for his firstborn.

"Dear, if we get a brand new HDB flat, it will take a while before we can move in. We must first register and then ballot. And we may not be successful at balloting. If we fail, then must try again. Even if we are lucky enough to be balloted, the flat needs a few years to be constructed. It's not like you want the flat next month, you can get it next month," Teng reasoned.

"Maybe we should buy a second-hand flat? It would be faster," suggested Siew Ling. "Think about it. If we buy directly from HDB, the estates tend to be in *ulu* places. We want to be more central, right? That means our flat must be in mature estates.

"Moreover, because a second-hand flat is already built and occupied, we can see who the neighbours are, the unit's actual facing, how close the market is, where the bus stops are, and so on. If it's new, we have to imagine how the flat will be like. And we are not very good at imagining.

"Remember when we bought this flat? It wasn't built yet and we had to imagine how the view was like from our floor, and how close the other blocks were. Aiyoh, a lot of unknowns leh. And if we imagine wrongly, we could be choosing the wrong flat."

"Hmm . . . I see your point. Let me talk to Peter and see what he says," replied Teng.

Railway Line 0 HDB Flat 1

Teng met Peter for dinner on a Monday evening. It was one of those days when Peter had more free time.

"Hey, Teng. Remember the real estate study that I told you about? The one the NUS professors studied about private property within 400 metres of the railway line?" Peter asked. "So the resale prices went up by about 3 percent when the news was first announced about stopping the train services. But now that the train lines have been removed, guess what? It drove prices up even further!"

"What?" Teng's eyes gleamed, "By how much? Quickly say."

"Hehehe . . .," laughed Peter as he toyed with Teng, prolonging the suspense. "You guess lah!"

"Eh . . . another 3 percent?" Teng hazarded.

"No, higher."

"Eh . . . 5 percent?" ventured Teng, not daring to raise his hopes too high.

"Between 6 to 7.5 percent!" Peter exclaimed. "You happy or not?"

Teng was dumbfounded and bewildered. This was way beyond his dreams. Maybe the cohort size effect that he and Peter heard about when they were in primary school wasn't there to haunt him anymore.

"Don't get too excited. The study was on 2,322 private houses located within 400 metres from the KTM railway line with a total value of almost $3 billion. With the removal of the railway line, it increased the value of the properties by about $360 million. Overall, prices went up by about 12 percent," explained Peter.

With the removal of the railway line, it increased the value of the properties by about $360 million. Overall, prices went up by about 12 percent.

"But there's a difference between resale value and new property value. These property developers are really one kind. They are very smart and they know how to take advantage of the good news.

"They made the first round when the news came out that the KTM railway line will be removed. Remember I told you that before? New houses went up by 8 to 12 percent based on just the announcement. Resale prices went up by 2 to 3.3 percent; much smaller than new houses but still better than nothing. These are the 'anticipative effects' because the railway tracks were still there. They weren't removed yet. It's just the announcement that pushed up sales.

"Now, after more than a year, the railway lines have finally been removed. Guess what? New housing prices shot up by another 12 to 17 percent! Crazy, right?

"Together, they can go up by almost 30 percent from the value before the announcement. That's the premium people are willing to pay for quietness. And property developers are so smart. They really know how to play up this 'peace and quietness' feature and make more money. No wonder they are so filthy rich.

"I wish I had bought one of these new houses before the announcement was made. Just put the downpayment and slowly make progress payments. Then subsell. I would have made money."

Peter shook his head in regret.

"Anyway, back to you, bro. The resale private property is a better indicator for you. Just now what I said was for new properties sold by developers.

"That same NUS study found that for resale private houses, the removal of the railway line — the event that really gives you peace and quiet — boosted the resale price by 6 to 7.5 percent. So including the anticipative effect of 3 percent, I say your humble HDB flat has gone up easily by 8 to 10 percent – not too shabby! Thank you Malaysia and Singapore *gahmen*," laughed Peter.

"But how come the appreciation for resale is lower than for new properties?" asked Teng.

"Who knows? Maybe the peace and quiet is sweeter in a new house than a resale house," laughed Peter as he rolled his eyes.

Superstitions

Some weeks later, Peter arranged with Teng and Siew Ling to view a few resale flats. They were looking at four- and five-room flats in Serangoon, Tiong Bahru and Queenstown – all mature estates. Unfortunately, there weren't any available in Dover near Fairfield Methodist School.

"Sorry, I tried. But it's hard to come by. I think people tend not to sell their flats when they know they are living near good schools, especially in areas with a lot of school-going children."

Siew Ling was excited. While living in Woodlands had its benefits of closeness to cheaper shopping and dining alternatives in Johor, she wanted to be closer to where the 'action' was – somewhere more central with easier access to other parts of Singapore. Moreover, she had heard that Malaysia might consider implementing GST. That would negate much of the benefits of shopping across the border.

But she was also mindful that the flat they were planning to buy should bring them good luck. She wouldn't want anything to jinx their young family, especially when it could be avoided.

She recalled how adorning Teng's dashboard with the small statuettes of the Goddess of Mercy, Buddha and the Jade Emperor, and hanging the crystal charm on the rear view mirror gave her a sense of assurance that Teng would be safe driving on the road.

She planned to do likewise when buying a property.

Growing up, she remembered listening to *Superstition* by Stevie Wonder:

When you believe in things that you don't understand
Then you suffer
Superstition ain't the way

"I hope I don't 'suffer' because of superstition. I want superstition to work for me, especially since buying a house costs a lot of money," worried Siew Ling.

Superstitious practices seem prevalent. In many countries, horoscopes remain a popular feature of newspapers, guiding readers. They commonly focus on the optimal times to make or avoid key financial decisions and transactions.

Even in countries ranked as highly educated, superstitious practices persist even when logic suggests that a more rational behaviour brought about by education should prevail over superstitions. Yet, people still believe in superstitions because they help them cope with misfortune and uncertainty as well as make sense of a complex world.

While superstitions might be seen at face value to be harmless quirks, they can influence decision making.

While superstitions might be seen at face value to be harmless quirks, they can influence decision making.

Superstitious beliefs endure if the probability of them being exposed as untrue is low. Unless there are some chances of a bad outcome when following superstitions and some chances of a good outcome when not practising them, an individual might never realise that they are untrue and continue to follow them.

No Go for 4

"Ok, guys. The first flat I'm showing you is at Mei Ling Street in Queenstown. It is near IKEA and Queensway Shopping Centre. There's also an MRT station but on the other side. The market here is quite good and you have dental and doctor clinics. So I should say this is a family-friendly neighbourhood. And Teng, you are into cars, right? There's a whole bunch of car dealers at Leng Kee, just a stone's throw away," explained Peter as he drove Teng and Siew Ling to their first viewing.

As they took the lift to the 14th floor, Siew Ling got a little anxious.

"Peter, 14th floor? *Yat say*? Definitely die?" said Siew Ling to Peter. "That's not an auspicious number."

Siew Ling was referring to the digits '1' and '4' in Cantonese. While '1' in Cantonese reads *yat* which also sounds like 'certainty', it was prefixed to '4' which in Mandarin as well as the Chinese dialects of Cantonese, Hokkien and Teochew sounds like 'death'. Therefore, '14' sounds like 'certain death' in Chinese.

On the other hand, '8' is auspicious because it sounds like 'prosperity' in Mandarin and Cantonese, but not in Hokkien or Teochew. But as most Singaporean Chinese know Mandarin, the association between '8' and prosperity is commonly known.

Although a house number has no intrinsic value, there is evidence of superstition among Chinese preferring the number '8' and disliking the number '4'. This belief seems to persist wherever in the world Chinese people are found.

Although a house number has no intrinsic value, there is evidence of superstition among Chinese preferring the number '8' and disliking the number '4'.

For instance, the government of Hong Kong has been selling new car license numbers by public auction. The prices of license numbers with the lucky '8' are higher than license numbers that include the unlucky '4'.

In neighbourhoods with relatively more Chinese residents in Vancouver, Canada, sales prices of houses with street address numbers ending in '4' were 2.2 percent lower than houses with other addresses. Conversely, those houses having street addresses ending in '8' were 2.5 percent more expensive than those without.

In Chengdu, China, apartments on floors with numbers ending in '8' were priced at almost 9 percent higher when sold as a resale but no differently when sold as new.

Even the Bank of China was influenced by superstitions as it opened its operations in Hong Kong on 8 August 1988. In another instance, the Beijing Olympics Games was officially opened at 8:08 pm on 8 August 2008.

"Keep an open mind. I'm not saying this is the flat for you. But it's good to compare the different features – layout, facing, renovated or not renovated," advised Peter.

Siew Ling was not comfortable. Though the flat was on a relatively high floor with a cool breeze, the ominous numbering (#14–24) was worrisome. *Yat say ee say* (1, 4, 2, 4) in Cantonese sounded very much like 'certainly will die and easy to die'.

She liked the layout though. Moreover, it had only been renovated just two years ago – she and Teng would not have to spend much before moving in – perhaps no more than the cost of applying a fresh coat of paint. But the anxiety owing to the possible pending bad luck gnawed at her. She raised her concerns to Teng and Peter.

"Maybe we can use that as a bargaining chip. Use number '14' to hammer down the price," suggested Teng to reassure her.

Since they were at Queenstown, Peter had scheduled them for a viewing of a flat in neighbouring Tiong Bahru. Tiong Bahru was known to them as a quaint neighbourhood with people congregating in a park to hear their pet birds sing, with a hawker centre well known for its local food including *chwee kueh* (a local Chinese snack made of flour and preserved radish) and a shop selling one of the best *kueh dada* (a Peranakan snack) in Singapore.

Although the flat they viewed was at least 60 years old, its winding staircase gave it an old charm which was quite appealing.

"Quite interesting. But to walk up three flights of stairs . . .," hesitated Siew Ling.

"This area is popular with the yuppies. On the one hand, they like the old architecture as it's a throwback to old Singapore. On the other hand, the neighbourhood has been spruced up to have very yuppie eateries," elaborated Peter.

Green Light for 8

The next flat they viewed was in Serangoon. It was located not too far from an underground MRT interchange station connected to Nex shopping mall. Although the unit was not on a high floor, there was a nice ring to its address.

"03–38 sounds good, don't you think?" enquired Siew Ling to Teng.

"*Leng sum sum fatt* sounds like 'birthing to prosperity'. Yah, that sounds good. And if I ever start a business, this number can also mean my business will prosper," responded Teng as he recited the address in Cantonese. "And it's near your favourite shopping centre, Nex."

They were walking along the common corridor to view the unit when a neighbour stepped out. Dressed in what seemed like a well-tailored white blouse and dark dress pants, along with a pearl and gold chain, the female neighbour was well-dressed, very much like a successful corporate person.

As they passed her unit, they glanced through an open window and saw a teenage girl dressed in a blue sleeveless uniform.

"Eh . . . the neighbour looks quite high-end," Siew Ling whispered to Teng.

"Yah. I think this is a good neighbourhood," Teng replied. "But the not-so-good thing is that the flat is on a low floor. Third floor is not exactly ideal, unless the lift breaks down. We also won't get the crosswinds for a good ventilation that the flats on higher floors will get. And there's no view."

"You can't have everything. There are always pros and cons. If you want everything, then you probably have to pay through your nose," added Peter. "Think of what is important to you. If having an auspicious number is very important so that you won't blame yourself for making a wrong choice once something bad happens, then features like no view are irrelevant.

"But if having a lucky address is nice to have but not a necessity, then you should consider prioritising the Queenstown and Tiong Bahru flats over this one."

Adding up the Numbers

After viewing the flats, Teng and Siew Ling were more conflicted than ever. There were so many considerations to think off; factors that were often times contradictory. With a limited budget, they had to compromise somewhere, somehow.

Together with Peter, they headed off to the hawker centre for some curry puffs and coffee.

"Thanks Peter for showing us the flats. We're so lost as to how to evaluate and decide. It's not easy," acknowledged Teng.

Siew Ling nodded in agreement and added, "I'm concerned about the address. I don't like '4' and much prefer '8'."

"I understand, Siew Ling. Some Singaporeans think like you too. So unit numbers with '4' are generally transacted at a lower price than those with '8'. Let me show you the transacted prices of houses with various unit numbers," said Peter as he went through his iPad and looked for the recent numbers.

[U]nit numbers with '8' fetch a higher price, followed by '2' and '6'. '4' fetches the lowest prices.

"As you can see here, unit numbers with '8' fetch a higher price, followed by '2' and '6'. '4' fetches the lowest prices.

"And you know, higher floors command a higher premium than lower floors. Look at this chart here," said Peter, directing them to another chart on housing prices for various floors.

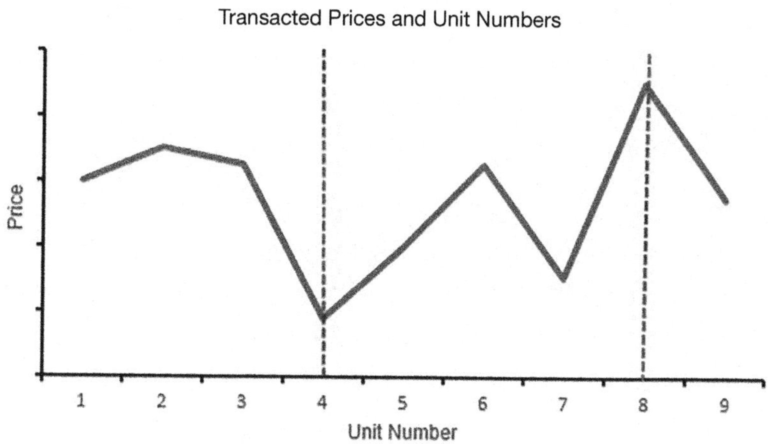

"The floors with '8' generally yield higher prices than other floors. So you need to set your priorities as to which is more important to you. There's always some give and take.

"Let me enlighten the both of you with this research that my real estate company did. It's confidential. So you don't tell anyone, because this information gives us leverage over our competitors," said Peter, trying to help them make a decision.

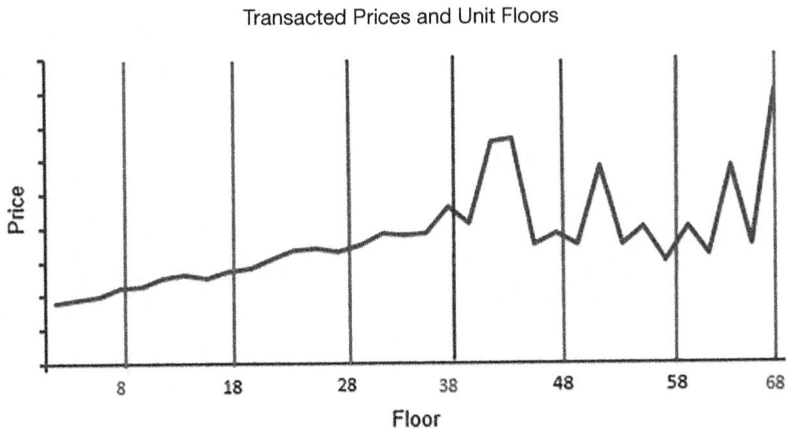

"I know numerology is important to you, or at least to Siew Ling. Nothing wrong with that. Different people have different priorities. It's what's comfortable with you that's important. So let me share this information with you.

"My boss was so impressed by the research done by the NUS professors who did the KTM railway line study that he asked them to find out how much numerology affects property prices in Singapore.

"The profs used several sources of data. From the Land Titles Registry, there's information on whether the property is freehold or leasehold, where it is located, the size as well as type of development — apartment, condo or landed. The database also reveals whether it is new, resale or subsale, its selling price, its mortgage status as well as who had bought and sold the property. Based on the name of the buyer/seller, one can also tell whether the individual concerned is Chinese, and *agak agak* (meaning 'guess') which dialect group he/she belongs to.

"The profs also retrieved the list of employees from the Singapore Government Directory. This allowed them to match the names to see whether the buyers are employed in the public sector.

"They also checked court records of civil actions pertaining to traffic accidents and linked them to property transactions.

"All in, more than 54,000 private property transactions were studied."

"Wow! So comprehensive," remarked Teng.

"Of course lah. This is NUS. These profs know what they are doing," replied Peter.

"But collecting data from traffic accident records and Singapore Government Employee Directory? I don't see the relevance," asked Siew Ling.

"I'll explain that later. You'll soon understand. It's quite ingenious," replied Peter. "But first, although we talked about superstitions driving property prices up or down, with people preferring '8' over '4', these professors think there might be something more to it. So they studied further."

Siew Ling and Teng listened attentively. The sharing was getting interesting.

"It turns out that maybe the preference for '8' could be an expression of conspicuous spending to signal to others that they can well afford it, rather than or in addition to superstitions," Peter explained.

[T]he preference for '8' could be an expression of conspicuous spending to signal to others that they can well afford it, rather than or in addition to superstitions.

"So, people might pay more for a number '8' to show that they can afford it, just like how they pay more to live in a more expensive neighbourhood or build a flashier home. A house in the prime district, District 10, costs more than an identical house in District 22, and this would show one's ability to pay for it. You pay a premium for bragging rights."

"Aiyah! Such a show off. *Atas* (meaning 'proud'). These people got too much money," sniffed Siew Ling. "And worse, they drive prices up for those who really believe in the number '8'."

"Peter, carry on. What did the profs find?" urged Teng, who had been curious about such matters ever since he was brought up with superstitious beliefs concerning being a Dragon baby.

"Aiyoh, I tell you, so interesting findings. Well, the profs studied by location – prime, not prime; north, south, east, west; and so on. They found that the very unlucky addresses are always the cheapest and those with very lucky addresses the most expensive.

"I think we expected that. Nothing startling there.

"Now, in Singapore, the government master plan stipulates the maximum height of each building. This varies across districts. Buildings with fewer than eight floors don't have many very lucky addresses compared to buildings with 40 floors. So in districts with relatively more short buildings, the supply of very lucky numbers is lower. Think about the Cavenagh area next to the Istana. For security reasons, high-rise apartments are not allowed. So there are even fewer lucky addresses in these locations.

"Also, you'll find that it's more difficult to find lucky addresses in the secondary market. Once people buy a lucky number house, they hold on to it. There's less than 12 percent of apartments with lucky numbers in the secondary market compared to 13.5 percent among brand new apartments.

"You know, the flat we saw at Serangoon with the number '8', that would be considered quite rare. So again, a premium for the lucky address."

Both Teng and Siew Ling nodded their heads. They had to seriously consider whether it was worth pursuing the Serangoon flat.

"Now, I ask you – Do you think it is only the Chinese who pay more for auspicious addresses?" asked Peter.

"Of course only the Chinese. Why would Indians or Malays bother about '8' and '4'?" replied Teng.

"Well, we found that for new sales, Chinese buyers pay 2.4 percent more for lucky addresses and 1.2 percent less for unlucky addresses. And this premium or discount also extends to subsales and resales in the secondary market.

"Look at it another way — the odds of a Chinese buying an apartment with a very lucky address as compared to other addresses is 20 percent higher than a non-Chinese person.

[T]he odds of a Chinese buying an apartment with a very lucky address as compared to other addresses is 20 percent higher than a non-Chinese person.

"But you know what? Non-Chinese buyers also pay a premium. In fact, they pay 1.3 to 3.6 percent more in general."

"Aahh . . . So strange. Are they Malays and Indians?" enquired Teng.

"Well, it turns out many of these non-Chinese are not Singaporeans, Peter revealed. "They are foreigners. Perhaps as foreigners, they may be at an information disadvantage relative to locals. So they *kena ketuk* (meaning 'got scammed').

"So the profs took out these foreigners from the study, re-analysed the data and found that numerology has little effect on non-Chinese Singaporeans. So Teng, you are right."

Conspicuous Consumption

"So what about the show-off effect you were talking about?" asked Siew Ling.

"Well, the professors were saying that the discount for an unlucky address can be viewed as the price that a buyer is willing to accept for potential bad luck in the future. On the other hand, the premium from a lucky address is the price that a buyer is willing to pay for potential good luck in the future.

"But because psychologically people don't like risks and want to avoid losses, the discount for unlucky addresses should be larger than the premium for lucky addresses. But the profs did not find that, which is inconsistent with the superstitious belief that unlucky addresses bring bad luck and lucky addresses good luck.

"So they asked my CEO, who has more than 25 years of real estate experience, what he thought. Now, my boss is quite smart. He suggested that conspicuous consumption may also explain why people pay a premium for lucky addresses. People spend more to signal status and wealth. But when it comes to unlucky addresses, paying at a discount doesn't signal lower status. So there's less effect on unlucky addresses.

"Well, the profs investigated this possible explanation. Remember earlier I mentioned that Chinese are 20 percent more likely to buy a lucky address than non-Chinese? The professors studied further and found out that such preferences are limited to only non-prime areas. Now, why do you think this is so?"

"Peter sounds like a teacher. He explains so systematically and confidently," thought Teng smilingly, thinking back to their childhood days when Peter was a loud kid who spoke his mind off.

Siew Ling who had been listening attentively replied, "Easy . . . because buying a home in a prime area is a luxury and is conspicuous in itself!"

"So clever," said Teng, admiring his loving wife.

"You're absolutely right," said Peter. "Buying a home in a luxury district is definitely a signal of wealth and status as these homes cost more than those in ordinary neighbourhoods. Therefore, there is no need to use an auspicious number to show off wealth. Everyone living there are wealthy.

"But in an ordinary neighbourhood, how do you show you are wealthy? By your house number. Pay more for a lucky address and people will know you are rich."

Buying a home in a luxury district is definitely a signal of wealth and status as these homes cost more than those in ordinary neighbourhoods. Therefore, there is no need to use an auspicious number to show off wealth.... [I]n an ordinary neighbourhood, how do you show you are wealthy? By your house number. Pay more for a lucky address and people will know you are rich.

"Wow! Peter, you know, I never thought research can be so interesting. I always thought these professors do mumbo-jumbo kind of research — things that I don't understand and don't care about.

"But now that you've explained it, it's so fascinating. Are there some more findings?" asked Teng.

"Absolutely. The study also showed that dialect group doesn't affect preferences. We used to think the Cantonese are more superstitious than the Hokkiens or Teochews, right? I think in Singapore, we are already so *chumpo* (meaning 'mixed') — there are so few pure blooded Cantonese or Hokkien. Also, with the emphasis on Mandarin, fewer and fewer Singaporeans can speak dialects. So rhyming numbers with Chinese dialect sounds is fast disappearing.

"Also, knowledge on the superstitious interpretations of '4', *say* (death), and '8', *fatt* (prosperity), are commonly known across dialect groups although they come from the Cantonese phonetic. So regardless of whether you are Cantonese, Hokkien or Teochew, you are equally as likely to prefer auspicious addresses.

"But you know what? Whether you have an *ang moh* (meaning 'Western') name or not matters."

Teng and Siew Ling were surprised. How could a Western name influence superstitious property purchases? They were intrigued.

"Here's a little bit of history lesson," Peter explained. "As a former British colony, English-educated people tend to earn relatively more and give Western names like Claire and John to their children. Economically comfortable, they also tend to be less engaged in conspicuous spending.

"And so we found that the odds of buying an apartment with a lucky address as compared to other addresses is 4.8 percent smaller for a buyer with a Western given name than buyers without a Western given name. After all, these *ang moh-fied* Singaporeans are more Westernised and less believing of Chinese numerological superstition. And as is consistent with their coming from an established background where conspicuous displays of wealth are frowned upon, they are not into lucky addresses."

"That means you, Peter. You were given an *ang moh* name by your parents," joked Teng.

"You crazy? If I come from an established family, I won't be a property agent," laughed Peter. "Of course with Singapore becoming so cosmopolitan, almost everyone now has a Western name. So this effect may diminish in years to come."

Teng was not only amazed at the NUS findings that made sense to him, but he was equally and pleasantly surprised that his childhood friend had matured and spoke well. Gone was his loud and brash demeanour. Peter had since grown up and was now able to articulate eloquently.

Peter continued, "We also found that age affects preferences for lucky addresses. Understandably, older buyers have a stronger preference for lucky numbers than middle-aged and younger buyers. This is likely because they are more superstitious. So Teng, your mother and father are likely to pay more for a lucky address than you. Luckily they did not come along to view the flats. But I think Siew Ling represents them!"

Everyone laughed.

"How about government employees? You said you would explain why they were being studied too," reminded Siew Ling.

"Ah yes," said Peter. "I must say our civil servants are quite *dit dit* (meaning 'straight'). We found that the odds of a senior-level government employee purchasing a very lucky address is 13 percent less than that of other buyers. Why? I think it's because public-sector employees are supposed to refrain from conspicuous spending."

"And how about the traffic accidents data? What's the linkage?" asked Teng.

Peter smiled. His friends had a good memory. "You know, we talked about numerology and superstition. People who are superstitious would want to avoid bad luck. So those who had bad luck may prefer lucky addresses to ward off more bad luck.

"Well, the professors tallied the traffic accidents data and found that buyers who had been *sway* (meaning 'cursed') enough to be a victim of a traffic accident prefer lucky addresses. Perhaps this is a way for them to cope with misfortune. Now you see the linkage?"

Siew Ling and Teng nodded. Indeed, it was quite smart and creative of the professors to study these possible explanations.

Social Integration

"Sorry, ah. I have one more question," asked Siew Ling. It had been a long day and she was getting tired. "I heard that if I want to live in a block that has many Chinese households already, I will have to pay extra?"

"Yes, it's based on demand and supply," replied Peter. "If there's demand to live in a block where there is already a very high proportion of say, Chinese households, it also means supply is scarce because there will be fewer non-Chinese households selling their flat.

"The COV (Cash over Valuation) may be high in such instances. COV is the difference between transaction price and valuation.

"HDB has an ethnic integration policy to ensure racial integration in a multiracial nation. So if a particular block has reached a certain percentage of Chinese occupants, there's no way you can buy a flat there unless you are a member of the ethnic minority.

"So say a block already has X percent of Chinese households," Peter further explained. "It hasn't quite reached the limit yet but is almost there. And there is a Chinese family who wants to buy a flat from a non-Chinese family located on the 18th floor with a nice number. That Chinese family would have to pay a premium or COV not only for the auspicious number but also for being in an area where there is strong cultural affinity."

"So how much more does one have to pay?" asked Siew Ling.

"Well, based on my past experience, they pay about 2.4 percent more for COV or $100 more per square metre."

By this time, they had finished their curry puffs and coffee. Teng and Siew Ling parted ways with Peter and headed home to think through which flat to make an offer to. There's much for the couple to consider.

WANT TO KNOW MORE?

This chapter is based on Sumit Agarwal, He Jia, Liu Haoming, Ivan P.L. Png, Sing Tien Foo and Wong Wei-Kang, "Superstition, Conspicuous Spending, and Housing Markets: Evidence from Singapore," (March 2016). Available at SSRN: https://ssrn.com/abstract=2416832 or http://dx.doi.org/10.2139/ssrn.2416832; and Sumit Agarwal, Choi Hyun Soo, He Jie and Sing Tien Foo, "Social Interactions and Segregation in Public Housing Neighbourhoods in Singapore," (2017). Working Paper, National University of Singapore.

CHAPTER 9

Circling Up

Peter came by the next day with more information to help Teng and Siew Ling come to a decision. He had gotten hold of a technical report on the effects of the Circle Line on housing values. He thought this would be interesting to Teng as the Serangoon flat they had looked at the previous day sits close to a Circle Line station.

The Circle Line is Singapore's fourth MRT line. Opened in stages in 2010 and 2012, it is a fully underground line, which made construction costs hefty.

The line complements the existing North–South and East–West lines by connecting them at various interchanges. This shortens the journey time of commuters who plan to travel from the northern part of Singapore to the eastern or western regions or vice versa. By transferring between lines at the interchanges, commuters can reach their destinations in a shorter time.

"Teng, I've this report for you. It uses the opening of the Circle Line to see whether the line enhances the value of properties located near its stations. You know the Serangoon flat we saw yesterday? It's no more than a 10-minute walk to Nex shopping mall, which is where the MRT station is. That station is also an interchange, which is important because it allows you to take more than just the Circle Line," emphasised Peter, making sure that Teng understood the relevance of the report to his house hunting.

"Here's the report. I've got to run now for a house viewing," said Peter hurriedly. "But please read it. It may help you make a decision."

Teng took a look at the 25-page report. For someone with a lacklustre 'O' level qualification, and who preferred watching car racing to reading, the report seemed like a thesis.

"Err . . . How to read, ah?" Teng thought. "I've got an idea. I'll pass it to Siew Ling. After all, she's the one who seems to be more interested in Serangoon than the other places."

Mulling Through

Siew Ling was not pleased when Teng dumped the report on her. She already had to look after their son, who kept her hands full. Going through the report felt like running a marathon. "This ought to be a joint effort," she thought. After all, they were buying *their* house, not her house.

Instead, Teng was engrossed in watching the latest Korean drama. He had caught the K-wave bug from Siew Ling.

So when Ethan was fast asleep, Siew Ling got Teng to switch off the TV set and sit down together with her to go through the report.

"Ok, the report says," read Teng out loud:

> "This study uses the opening of the new Circle Line (CL) MRT stations in stages between 2010 and 2012 as the

> treatment events to empirically test the capitalisation effects of the CL project on housing prices."

"What does that mean?" Teng shook his head. He continued reading:

> "Like many previous studies, we use the hedonic model to empirically quantify the accessibility premiums associated with the new CL. One methodological challenge facing this type of empirical works is to resolve possible endogeneity problems in the housing price discovery process. New MRT projects bring more commercial developments and employment opportunities to areas surrounding new MRT stations. . . ."

"What the . . .," Teng didn't want to complete the colourful expression. "What is 'hedonic'? What is 'endogeneity'? Why do these people write like that? They speak English or not? Aiyoh, dear, do you understand?"

"Don't get so *manjang* (meaning 'irritable'). Stay calm," said an even-keeled Siew Ling. "I think we should try our best to read and for those parts that we understand, we understand. For those parts that we don't understand, we can try to figure it out by making sense out of it. Worse comes to worst, we can always ask Peter."

Siew Ling continued reading, and jotted down notes along the margins. Teng, in the meantime, had already checked out. Frustrated with not understanding the report and tired from the long hours of driving, his head slumped on Siew Ling's shoulder.

"The report says they studied houses located within 400 metres from the Circle Line stations," said Siew Ling as she patiently digested every line of the report.

"They found that the opening of the Circle Line increases the value of the houses located within 400 metres of its stations. These houses sell at an average price of 13 percent more compared to houses more than 400 metres away.

[T]he opening of the Circle Line increases the value of the houses located within 400 metres of its stations. These houses sell at an average price of 13 percent more compared to houses more than 400 metres away.

"There were about over 6,500 property transactions done during the period they were studying. The average selling price was $1.4 million for a total of $9.3 billion. The report also says that the opening of the Circle Line increased the total value of the houses within the 400-metre radius by $1.2 billion.

"Whoo! That's a lot."

As Siew Ling carried on reading, she remarked, "Dear, dear, wake up. Listen to this," as she elbowed Teng to check in.

"Over here in the report, it says that the increase is more for developer's new sale market *and* for HDB upgraders. *Alamak*! That means the Serangoon flat that we saw yesterday."

[T]he increase in prices is higher for houses that were previously not served by an MRT until the Circle Line came along. Those that were already served by an existing MRT station did not go up by as much.

As she continued reading, she said, "Wait... *Heng* ah! I don't think the Serangoon flat has gone up by so much. Because it says that the increase in prices is higher for houses that were previously not served by an MRT until the Circle Line came along. Those that were already served by an existing MRT station did not go up by as much.

"The Serangoon station is an interchange. There was already the North-East Line before the Circle Line. So that means that having the Circle Line there is beneficial but not as beneficial to places where there was no MRT station before. So the price increase is more for properties that never had an MRT station near them. Really *heng*. So the Serangoon flat did not go up too much in price."

Siew Ling felt good that with patience she could slowly decipher the technical report. She just hoped she had interpreted it correctly.

"And it also says that the price increase largely came about after the stations were opened. There was very little 'anticipative effect'," Siew Ling read slowly, stretching out the word 'an-ti-ci-pa-tive'.

"Eh, I've heard of this term before . . . 'anticipative effect' . . . where ah?" Siew Ling nudged Teng as his head propped on her shoulders.

"Wake up, wake up," she said a little louder, pushing him sideways. "What is 'anticipative effects'? I remember hearing that term before but can't remember where."

"Hmm . . . anticipative effects . . . anticipative effects . . .," said a blurry Teng as he tried to recall. "Yes. Peter used that term when he told us about the removal of the KTM railway line. There was a large anticipative effect as house prices went up after the announcement but before the railway tracks were actually removed because people anticipated there would be a positive effect on housing with the disappearance of the tracks."

"Ah yes, now I recall," said Siew Ling as she remembered how excited Peter was in telling Teng and her that they had *fatt* with the KTM Railway announcement. "So in the case of the Circle Line, that did not happen. Even though people knew where the stations would be, they did not raise their selling prices until the stations were operational. So why is this different from the KTM situation? Got to ask Peter."

WANT TO KNOW MORE?

This chapter is based on Diao Mi, Fan Yi and Sing Tien Foo, "A New Mass Rapid Transit (MRT) Line Construction and Housing Wealth: Evidence from the Circle Line," *Journal of Infrastructure, Policy and Development*, Vol. 1 (1), (2017), pp. 64–89.

CHAPTER 10

Tolls and Trolls

"Peter, thanks for the report on the Circle Line," said Siew Ling. Peter was bringing Teng and her to see more flats that day.

"It was not easy understanding the technical report. So *cheem*. I wish you were there to explain it to us in plain English," said Teng candidly.

"Sorry lah. These research reports are always technical because they have all these statistics and all. But if you go beyond all these *cheem* stuff, you can see how relevant the research is," explained Peter.

"We need to ask you this — do you know why there were no anticipative effects on housing prices for the Circle Line, but there were for the KTM Railway?" asked Siew Ling.

"You mean why the prices didn't go up upon the news of where the Circle Line MRT stations would be while the housing prices shot up the moment it was announced that the KTM Railway would be removed?" clarified Peter.

"Yup."

"Well, I think somehow for the Circle Line, there were less sentiments involved. This is only my conjecture. My gut feel is that for KTM Railway, it affected the Woodlands heartlanders. They were disturbed by the train noises. So knowing that the railway tracks would be gone soon made them happy – something to look forward to. There were emotions involved. So that boosted the home prices immediately.

"As for why this didn't happen for the Circle Line, I think there are a few reasons. First, I think there are quite a number of private housing estates near where some of the stations would be located. For instance, in the prime Bukit Timah area where the Farrer Road, Botanic Gardens and Caldecott stations are designated as future sites, there were a sizeable number of private properties. People living in these prime landed properties might not need the MRT as they owned cars. In fact, some might not even want an MRT station near their homes for fear of having more people walking around their area. Quite unfounded of course.

"Second, Singapore has, by and large, a comprehensive public bus system that gets you to various parts of Singapore quite easily. So I think residents around would-be stations were contented with existing public transportation. They might not have realised the value of a new MRT station until its opening. Only after the station is opened do they appreciate the connectivity and convenience between the train and the bus, and how much they could save on travelling time.

"But of course these are just what I think."

"Hmm . . . It seems logical. And to think that these technical reports are so useful to us. Such research are about our daily lives and help us to make decisions. I never knew that research can be so relevant and useful," appreciated Siew Ling.

One Down

Peter brought them to view more flats. But the flats were no better. They were, in fact, worse than the three they had seen on their first house hunting day.

With Ethan fast growing up, Teng knew he had to find a new home soon. Yet, buying a home was a highly involving matter. He did not want to make a wrong decision that would haunt him for a very long time.

There were so many considerations to account for, though the most pressing were financial considerations and location. All three flats – Queenstown, Tiong Bahru and Serangoon – satisfied the location criterion. But the exact address and the walk-up feature affected their finances.

The Tiong Bahru flat was a throwback to the old days which Teng knew his parents would love. Moreover, the many eateries there appealed to him and would be useful when his mother or Siew Ling were too tired to cook. But with his ageing parents moving in to help look after Ethan, a walk-up flat might not be that ideal. A fall on the stairs for the elderly folks might spell more headaches down the road.

After several nights of tossing and turning, Teng and Siew Ling decided to strike this flat off their list even though they believed they could have bargained for a lower price because of the walk-up stairs.

Teng called up Peter. "Hey, Peter. After much thought, Siew Ling and I are not interested in the Tiong Bahru flat. I can't see my elderly parents walking up and down three flights of stairs every day. Some may say it's a good exercise but if one of them falls, that would be very problematic for us."

"That's sensible," said Peter. "But seriously, think carefully through the Queenstown and Serangoon flats. They are great buys. But decide fast as when they are good, they will get snapped up faster than the others. You don't want to lose this opportunity and later regret."

Electronic Road Pricing Bargaining Chip

Teng was hoping that Peter could help them bring the prices down for the other two flats. He was quietly confident that the Queenstown flat on the 14th floor could be bargained further. After all, Peter did say that according to the NUS report, people pay a little less for properties with unlucky addresses.

But looking at Siew Ling's sombre face when viewing the Queenstown flat, he knew deep down his wife would be reluctant to live at an unlucky address even if the price were right. But living in Queenstown would have its benefits – it was not only convenient to go to Orchard Road but also to Fairfield Methodist School where Teng intended to enrol Ethan in. But Teng knew that the latter would be a fantasy since they did not qualify on the grounds of distance proximity.

"Peter, I'm asking you to talk to the sellers and negotiate a lower price for us. I know Siew Ling has reservations about the Queenstown flat because of the number '14'. But if you can bargain down to a price that she cannot refuse, I think there is a good chance that that's the house for us.

"And bargain also for the Serangoon flat. I know Siew Ling like that unit. But expensive leh. Can you bargain because it is on a low floor? We want the best deal. You know me. I'm not only *kiasu* but I'm also *kiabor* (meaning 'scared of wife'). Use your bargaining expertise for your good friend lah," begged Teng.

"Of course, I'll try my best. How long have we been friends, bro? You know I'll do whatever I can," replied Peter. "But be mindful. Even though the NUS study showed that on average, unlucky addresses are sold for lower value, it's only 1 or 2 percent less, if at all. So don't get your hopes up.

"As for the Serangoon unit, the address is auspicious. It doesn't matter whether you believe in it or not. As long as the market says it's a lucky address, a lucky address it is.

"It is also near the Circle Line MRT station. And that station also serves as an interchange.

"The seller is using these as its selling strengths. It's tough to use low floor as a bargaining tool over lucky number, especially with its proximity to the MRT station. The seller may tell you to 'go fly kite' (meaning 'get lost').

"And although this unit just came on to the market, my contacts have told me that there are already several interested buyers. That may just up the price further if you don't offer soon.

"I'm not pressurising you but just saying it as it is."

"I see," Teng furrowed his eyebrows. He thought for more reasons to bargain down the Serangoon flat.

"How about ERP? I read in the papers that when the ERP rates went up, there was a drop in real estate prices in areas bounded by ERP gantries.

"Although the Serangoon flat is not within ERP area, we can say that I drive to work and the tolls outside Serangoon will cause me to fork out more for driving. That will make the Serangoon flat less attractive."

"Huh? ERP?" Peter said in amusement. "Nice try, Teng. But you sound like a drowning man grasping at straws. Bringing in ERP to bargain? You've got to be kidding. This is the first time I've heard of it. But I give you full marks for trying."

"Hey, I try lah. I'm thinking of any logical reason to make the seller bring down his price," justified Teng.

Peter laughed.

[W]hen the ERP prices were raised ... property prices went down by 19 percent in CBD, Central Business District, relative to those outside CBD.

"Let me explain the findings to you. That study was conducted when the ERP prices were raised by $1. Yes, the newspapers reported that when it happened, property prices went down by 19 percent in CBD, Central Business District, relative to those outside CBD.

"But this was for retail real estate within the ERP area — Orchard Road, Bugis and Marina. The Serangoon flat is residential, not retail, and neither is it within CBD.

"In fact, for commercial and residential properties within CBD, there was negligible effect on transacted prices."

Teng groaned.

"The study which used data from the Urban Redevelopment Authority did not include HDB flats because there are very few of such flats in CBD," continued Peter. "The researchers coded the exact location of each ERP gantry. Each building is coded as either within the cordoned area or outside using its postal code. This way, the researchers can assess whether a property transaction was within or outside CBD and whether it was for a retail building or a private residence.

"Altogether, there were over 19,000 transactions within CBD and 15,000 outside CBD for private residences and retail properties.

"So I'm afraid Teng, you cannot use ERP as a bargaining chip. The seller will laugh at both of us and we'll look so stupid.

"Give me a few days. I'll try my best and get back to you when I hear from the sellers."

Hungry Ghost Bargaining Chip

Peter came back with nothing. Both sellers were stubborn and refused to budge.

Teng and Siew Ling were exasperated. It looked like they might have to borrow from Teng's parent to buy a bigger flat. Teng was planning for his parents to rent out their flat and earn some passive income after moving in with them. With Teng covering the extra food and utilities bills, his parents might be able to spare some cash.

Teng thought of yet another strategy to ease their finances.

"Hey, Peter. How about this? I've my HDB flat to sell also. Why don't I sell my flat now and buy later during the Hungry Ghost month? Very few people want to buy during the Chinese seventh month, right? Prices will be reduced. So I buy low, sell high. Just like in the stock market," said Teng with a devilish smile, pleased with himself for coming up with what he thought was a brilliant timing strategy.

"And if you think we have no place to stay for the time being, we can cram into my parents' flat for a few months just so we get the best deal both ways," added Teng, in anticipation to Peter's objection. "That's my kind of 'anticipative effect'," Teng laughed in reference to the KTM Railway study which Peter had told them about some years ago.

Lunar Seventh Month

Like the Americans have Halloween, the Chinese have the month-long Hungry Ghost festival during the seventh month of the lunar calendar, usually in mid-August to mid-September, when supposedly the gates separating the realms of hell from the living open.

For Taoists, there are taboos to be avoided during the Hungry Ghost month which include not going out at night, keeping doors closed, and avoiding buying, renovating and moving houses during the month. Superstitions surrounding the Hungry Ghost month lead people to put off home purchases.

During this period, Chinese families make offerings to their deceased ancestors, hoping that wandering spirits appeased with the food offerings and prayers would not cause mischief to homes and work places.

For Taoists, there are taboos to be avoided during the Hungry Ghost month which include not going out at night, keeping doors closed, and avoiding buying, renovating and moving houses during the month. Superstitions surrounding the Hungry Ghost month lead people to put off home purchases.

Peter's Advice

"Really, Teng?" said Peter not believing what he just heard from Teng; to time the selling of his Woodlands home and purchase of a new flat to fit the Hungry Ghost month.

"I wouldn't advise that. What if you sell your flat now but can't find a suitable one to buy when seventh month comes? Then you're stuck. You think you can *tahan* (meaning 'tolerate') staying at your parents' place for so long? And what if prices keep going up? Then you'll really be losing your pants. You don't want to be caught by mistiming.

"Anyway, it is not true that during the Hungry Ghost month, there is dampened interest in the property market."

"Really?" said a surprised Teng. "I've always thought transaction volume is down during the seventh month."

Peter explained, "Over a 10-year period covering more than 82,000 non-landed private property transactions, the seventh month transactions have in fact been quite strong. On average, the lunar seventh month recorded sales of slightly over 8,500 units. Contrary to belief, the fifth, sixth and seventh lunar months were the most active in terms of the number of transactions, followed by quite a sharp fall in the eighth through to the 10th month.

[T]he lunar seventh month recorded sales of slightly over 8,500 units. Contrary to belief, the fifth, sixth and seventh lunar months were the most active in terms of the number of transactions, followed by quite a sharp fall in the eighth through to the 10th month.

"Wait a minute while I see whether I can find the chart for you in my iPad," Peter said as he rummaged his messenger bag. With some swiping of his finger, Peter soon found the chart he was referring to.

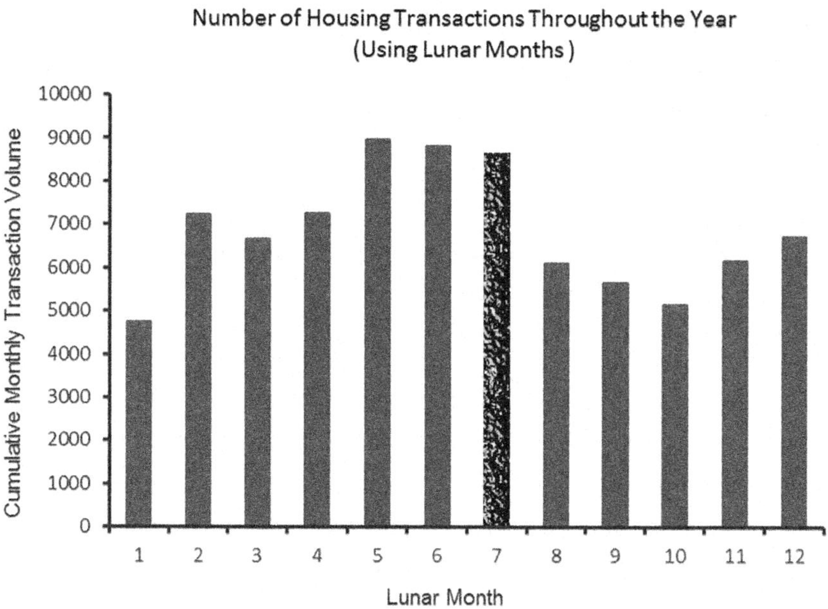

[T]he strong sales during seventh month is because non-superstitious buyers including non-superstitious Chinese buyers, do not think it's a taboo to buy property. They find plenty of good bargains during this period when superstitious Chinese buyers stay away.

"See?" Peter pointed out as he showed him the chart.

"How come, leh?" said a quizzical Teng. "It doesn't make sense."

"Maybe everyone is thinking like you, Teng," laughed Peter.

"Here I go again. I have to give him a lecture backed with facts so that he understands and believes," thought Peter.

"Actually, the strong sales during seventh month is because non-superstitious buyers, including non-superstitious Chinese buyers, do not think it's a taboo to buy property. They find plenty of good bargains during this period when superstitious Chinese buyers stay away. There's less competition.

"Having said that, prices do fall during Hungry Ghost month. In the resale market, prices go down by slightly over 10 percent compared to other months. But if you were buying a brand new home from the developer, it will be about 8 percent cheaper.

"So yes, prices do fall. But it's a risk because the non-superstitious buyers are coming in to compete against you and like I said earlier, you may not get what you want.

"I think the more savvy sellers will withhold selling choice properties during that month. They know their property is desired. Why sell at a lower price during the one month when prices are dampened? It's only one month. It doesn't make sense for them not to wait. So, you are likely to see more of the less desired properties in the market during Hungry Ghost month."

Peter continued, "Generally, people will sell their home and buy another about the same time so that they don't get caught should the market turn.

"You said you are *kiasu*. If indeed you are, you shouldn't be buying and selling at different times.

"And friend, you said you *kiabor*. Really? Siew Ling is so superstitious. Yet, you dare to go against her wishes and buy a house during Hungry Ghost month?" Peter laughed.

Teng thought through. What Peter said made sense. Going through an early sale of his flat and a later purchase during Hungry Ghost month would require perfect timing with too many unknowns. Siew Ling would be very anxious because of the uncertainties, not to mention himself too. If he were to make the wrong decision, he would hear no end from her.

Moreover, moving his household things not once but twice – first to his parents' place and later to the new home – could be backbreaking with a young kid in tow. Besides who would know how long they would have to stay at his parents' small flat.

Even if he found a storage place to put his things, it would still require additional work. Furthermore, the storage costs could end up being costly, negating any savings, especially if he's unable to find a cheaper desirable flat during the Hungry Ghost month.

There were just way too many uncertainties for Teng to sleep well at night.

"Thanks, Peter. I hear you. You're right. The timing must be *choon*. Please look out for a buyer for our flat too. I don't want to be stuck with two properties," said Teng.

WANT TO KNOW MORE?

This chapter is based on Sumit Agarwal, Mo Koo Kang and Sing Tien Foo, "Impact of Electronic Road Pricing on Real Estate Prices in Singapore," *Journal of Urban Economics*, Vol. 90, (2015), pp. 50–59; Sumit Agarwal and Sing Tien Foo, "The 'Hungry Ghost Month Effect' on Housing," *The Straits Times*, (2 September 2015). www.straitstimes.com/opinion/the-hungry-ghost-month-effect-on-housing; and Sumit Agarwal and Sing Tien Foo, "Hungry Ghosts and Home Prices," (2 September 2015). http://thinkbusiness.nus.edu/article/hungry-ghosts-and-house-prices/

CHAPTER 11

New House, New Friends

Teng and Siew Ling ended up purchasing the Serangoon flat. Peter managed to sell their Woodlands flat at a good price given the appreciation with the removal of the KTM railway line. Together with some savings that they had scraped together over the years, they could afford the Serangoon flat.

With Siew Ling's concern for a trouble-free life, she consulted a geomancer for an auspicious date to move in. She also had a priest to chant the rites and bless the home.

With this move, Siew Ling had to look for a job nearer to their new home. Eventually, she found employment as a sales assistant for another shoe store at Nex, a shopping mall within walking distance.

But she missed not shopping in JB. However, she consoled herself that any advantages to cross-border shopping would soon be gone, since there were rumours that the Malaysian government was going to impose GST.

Ma and Pa moved in a few months later. They had taken a little more time because they were reluctant to leave their neighbours whom they had known for the last 30 years. But they understood that family came first – they were needed to help look after Ethan while both Teng and Siew Ling were at work.

After they shifted in, Teng helped them spruce up their old flat for tenancy. Giving the walls a fresh coat of paint, the old dame had a new lease of life.

Peter was again helpful. Having sold Teng's flat and helped him buy the Serangoon unit, here was another opportunity to make commission – renting out the elderly couple's flat.

Not too long thereafter, all were under one roof.

The Neighbours

Teng and Siew Ling had bumped into the corporate lady neighbour whom they had chanced upon a few months ago when they were house viewing. They exchanged smiles and were cordial. Very few words were exchanged except for the cursory "Hello" and a smile.

They did get her name though – Josephine, or Josie for short. She has a teenage daughter, Sarah.

After seeing Josie walk to the MRT station a few times, Teng plucked up the courage to talk to her under the guise of a neighbourly cab driver offering her a ride to a convenient destination.

He soon learnt that Josie works in the Corporate Planning & Development department of the Land Transport Authority (LTA). It turned out that Josie believed very much in saving the environment. Hence, she tried to take public transport on most occasions even though Teng believed she could well afford a car.

One day, Siew Ling brought a pot of Ma's winter melon soup over to Josie's home. Overwhelmed by the kind gesture, Josie invited the neighbours on both sides of her flat to her house for dinner. That's where Teng and Siew Ling met Professor Sing, a lecturer in NUS, and his family.

With a quiet smile and a humble demeanour, Professor Sing talked about his ongoing research projects.

"At NUS, research is very important. And it's not just any research. We aim for quality. And the research must ideally impact the society," Professor Sing explained.

"May I ask what research projects are you engaging in now?" enquired Josie.

"There are a few at various stages. There's one on the cooling property measures and how that might affect how people spend," replied Professor Sing.

"I'm curious. I just bought my flat and I'm keen to know how it may affect my spending," asked Teng.

"Ah yes. You are affected by the cooling measures," nodded Professor Sing. "We found that six months after the cooling measures were instituted, homeowners' total debit and credit card spending went down.

"Most of the reduction came from credit card spending. Homeowners reduced their spending on credit cards by almost 60 percent, whereas debit card spending remained virtually unchanged.

[S]ix months after the cooling measures were instituted, homeowners' total debit and credit card spending went down.... [H]omeowners with a low credit card limit reduced their spending by an additional 33 percent more than those with high credit limits.

"We also found that homeowners with a low credit card limit reduced their spending by an additional 33 percent more than those with high credit limits. What this means is that the policy change has a greater effect on credit-constrained homeowners who face a higher risk of running into costly card debt."

"So what should I do? What's your advice?" asked Siew Ling.

"Well, I'm no finance expert but I'd suggest that you plan and manage your household spending carefully since you have limited access to your home equity and you cannot release the wealth tied up in your flat," advised Professor Sing. "I also see such cooling measures as a possible tool that the government can use to moderate consumption and control for inflation and influence economic growth."

After a short pause, Professor Sing continued, "But the research project that I'm really keen on is on water conservation. It is mind-boggling how much water Singaporeans use."

"Ohh . . . That's interesting. I'd be interested to know more about that," said Josie who was not only thinking about how much water Sarah used when she took a shower but was very much into environmental protection herself.

"Well," hesitated Professor Sing. "Singaporeans are using a lot of water. That's all I can say for now as the research is still ongoing."

Changing the topic, Professor Sing turned to Sarah, "Sarah, which grade are you in now?"

Sarah, a teenager, was feeling quite awkward. At an age where she felt she did not quite fit in, she gave a terse reply, "Sec 3."

"Wow! Next year will be an important year then," Teng joined in with reference to the 'O' level exams that Sarah would be taking the following year.

"And Josie, you must be preparing for the 'O' levels too?" he joked, knowing that *kiasu* parents would be buying lots of past-year exam papers for their children to practise for the big exam.

"No lah. I leave her be. What would I know about Physics and Chem now. I've given all that back to my teachers a long time ago," came Josie's quick reply.

The older people at the dining table laughed. They identified with what Josie said. They had all forgotten what they had learnt in school.

"I outsource all the teaching to private tutors. Better they teach than me. I think teaching your own child can make your blood boil," explained Josie as she referred to her impatience when teaching Sarah.

The private tuition industry is huge in Singapore. The Household Expenditure Survey found that families spent $1.1 billion a year in 2012/13 on tuition, almost double the $650 million spent in 2004 and $820 million spent in 2009. In another study, it was found that seven out of 10 parents send their children for tuition. This parental behaviour has led to a burgeoning of tuition providers. Some parents spend several hundreds or thousands of dollars on tuition each month, even though the extent to which tuition helps in improving their children's academic performance is questionable. While this may be an indication of Singapore's culture of valuing education, it also reflects a *kiasu* mentality. When it comes to their children's education, Singaporean parents fear losing out.

Teng remembered how much he had not liked studying in his student days — although on hindsight, he realised he should have worked harder and spent less time playing with marbles. He vowed to make sure that Ethan would not make the same mistake.

"Josie, sorry if I sound rude. I'm curious why you take public transport to work. Is it because you want to know firsthand how it is like to take public transport? Then you can improve the bus and the train systems? I would think it is more convenient to drive to work. Saves time," Teng enquired probingly.

"Truth be told, I'm scared of driving. Ironic, isn't it? I work for the transport authority but am scared of driving," laughed Josie.

"It's true I get a first-hand feel of our public transport system by using it every day. That helps in setting policies and knowing whether they are effective.

"But I'm also a green supporter. Our public transport system is world class. We can get from one place to another quite quickly. And Singapore is so small compared to America or Australia. Nothing is too far.

"Why should we contribute to traffic congestion, air pollution and noise pollution when there's already an existing public transport system that can get you from Point A to Point B quite easily?

"The other day, Sarah and I went to Marina Bay Sands to watch *Beatlemania On Tour*. It was easy to get there. Just take the Circle Line and we're there in no time.

"And car prices are so high. I don't want to spend money on a depreciating asset," Josie said, while being mindful that her neighbours drove.

To bolster her case on Singapore's superior public transport system, Josie added, "For example, at LTA, we offer early bird free rides for journeys on MRT entering into the CBD area before 7:45 am on weekdays. We do this to reduce the peak period crowd so that everyone can have a comfortable ride. Those who go to work earlier benefit from a free ride. I think it's good that LTA thinks of ways to benefit commuters and make public transportation better."

"Hmm . . . That reminds me of a study my NUS colleagues at the Business School did. They studied travel behaviour on buses and trains using data from EZ-link cards. Josie, you might have heard of their findings as this study was collaborated with LTA," declared Professor Sing.

EZ-Link Cards

The EZ-Link card, issued by LTA, is a stored value contactless smart card used mainly for paying public transport fares — be it bus, MRT or light rail — in Singapore. Introduced in 2002, such cards not only alleviated the burden of carrying the correct change for fares, but they also made for speedier boarding times. Commuters tap their cards on the reader when they board and alight from buses, or when they enter and leave MRT stations. While cash payment is still possible for commuters, a higher fare is charged then. The EZ-Link card is similar to the Octopus card in Hong Kong and the Touch 'n Go card in Malaysia.

Timing Reliability of Public Transport

"My colleagues wanted to find out whether public transit riders look to save travel time and how much they value schedule reliability in public transportation. And you can tell this by how they travel — do they change from bus to train in order to save time and so on.

"So they analysed the travel patterns of about 4 million cardholders over one month. I think there were over 175 million trips studied for buses and MRT trains. It was really a massive project.

"They found that in general, travel time reliability is important. This means people want the buses and trains to arrive and leave on schedule.

My colleagues wanted to find out whether public transit riders look to save travel time and how much they value schedule reliability in public transportation. And you can tell this by how they travel — do they change from bus to train in order to save time ...

"But because different modes of public transport have varying levels of reliability, this may waste commuter time waiting for say, a bus to come. The bus may be late or come too early and the passenger misses it and has to wait 10 minutes for the next one. In which case, some commuters may be more willing to switch to another transportation mode, say the MRT train which is more reliable, to save commuting time.

"So my colleagues studied the different groups of commuters — children/students, adults, and senior citizens. And they could tell who belongs to which group by the type of card used — concession or non-concession.

"They found that adult passengers place higher value on travel time than senior citizens and children/students. They change to different transport modes more frequently to shorten their travel time. But still, compared to private car drivers, such public transit commuters value time saving less so.

"So, Josie, I think you've got more time to spare than car drivers since you are willing to take public transport."

"No," retorted Josie emphatically to support her stand while protecting her ego. "I can do my work while I'm on the train while you can't do that when you're driving. So I'm actually valuing my time more so than drivers."

Professor Sing continued, "This finding is important to LTA. My colleagues found that for travels involving CBD, reliability is important. I guess CBD journeys tend to be work-related. One must not be late for work or for appointments. So public transport into CBD and within CBD must be on schedule."

Josie nodded, mentally taking down notes as she took in these findings.

"And Josie, I think you'll find this one very insightful. It's whether commuters value fare or travel time more so.

"My colleagues found that for adult passengers, travel time is more important than how much the fare is. If buses can improve their schedule reliability, more adult commuters will switch to buses. For children, students and senior citizens, they don't really care about schedule reliability."

[A]dult passengers who are the majority of morning peak hour travellers are somewhat insensitive to fares. So the early bird discount is likely to be ineffective with this group of commuters. For them, service reliability is more important.

Professor Sing continued, "So Josie, you mentioned just now about LTA having the early bird free MRT ride for those going into CBD. The problem is, adult passengers who are the majority of morning peak hour travellers are somewhat insensitive to fares. So the early bird discount is likely to be ineffective with this group of commuters. For them, service reliability is more important. So things like the bus-only lanes during peak hours that will improve timing appeal better to them than discounted fares."

"Professor Sing may have a point there. I'd better check out this report and study it more before bringing it up to my boss," thought Josie, telling herself that she should do this later that week before her meeting with her boss. After all, she wanted to impress him to facilitate a promotion.

Small Talk

Teng was quite overawed by his illustrious neighbours. He felt a little bit unsure of himself, but he thought, "Hey, I always have to start somewhere."

Despite them being far better educated than he was, he found them to be extremely friendly. He even thought of introducing Professor Sing to Peter as both shared the same interest in real estate. Perhaps they would hit off given their common interest. It's about time to return Peter a favour after he had tried so hard to get him and Siew Ling their new flat and sell their old one at a great price.

"What do you do during your spare time, Teng?" asked Josie.

"Not much, unfortunately," said Teng, as he tried hard to form the next few sentences in proper English without saying "lah", "mah" or "hor". He would have to learn from Peter.

"I spend almost all my time driving. I used to have a co-driver. But now I have the taxi to myself and thus do all the driving. I drive Siew Ling where she needs to go. And now with Ethan growing up, I drive my family to places of interest. Also I drive my parents to the polyclinic to see the doctor. The only driving I don't do is driving people up the wall!"

This time, everyone including the children laughed. Teng was being hilarious and he liked the attention. He thought he probably made a good impression. At least they understood his humour.

"Uncle Teng, are you still able to find passengers easily, now that there's Über?" asked Sarah. As a digital native, she has the Über app on her mobile phone. Once, when she was out with her mum and they needed a cab, none were to be found. But with her Über app, she found a private car for hire within a short time. That impressed Josie, which led her to install the Über app on her phone.

"Still ok. So far, it's the more tech savvy people who are using Über. Older people still prefer to call for a taxi. But I signed up to be a Grab driver too. Grab is Über's competitor. So I still get some business from these ride-hailing companies. It's not so bad," was Teng's response, although it gnawed at him that this scenario might soon change against him.

"What about you, Josie? What do you do during your spare time? Work at LTA must be tough, especially now with the train breakdowns," asked Siew Ling.

"Yes, that's true," nodded Josie. "A breakdown means the team will have to work overtime. But you know, we just have to keep on improving and have frequent maintenance. You know how in Singapore we always pride ourselves to be world class.

"So I relax over the weekend with a game of golf. I find that very therapeutic."

The evening went by quite quickly. Teng and Siew Ling were pleased that their decision to buy the Serangoon unit had turned out to be the right one.

WANT TO KNOW MORE?

This chapter is based on Sumit Agarwal and Qian Wenlan, "Access to Home Equity and Consumption: Evidence from a Policy Experiment," *The Review of Economics and Statistics*, Vol. 99(1), (2017), http://www.mitpressjournals.org/doi/abs/10.1162/REST_a_00606?journalCode=rest; and Sumit Agarwal, Diao Mi, Jussi Keppo and Sing Tien Foo, "Public Transit Riders' Preferences for Travel-Time Savings and Reliability: Evidence from Smart Card Transactions in Singapore," (2017). Working Paper, National University of Singapore.

Other materials came from Amelia Teng, "Tuition Industry Worth Over $1b a Year," *The Straits Times*, (25 December 2016). www.straitstimes.com/singapore/education/tuition-industry-worth-over-1b-a-year/; "The Factors which have Contributed to the Tuition Industry Boom in Singapore," www.economicscafe.com.sg; and "1 Billion Spent on Tuition in One Year," *AsiaOne Online*, (9 November 2014). www.nie.edu.sg/news-detail//1-billion-spent-on-tuition-one-year

CHAPTER 12

Lady, Do You Want to Tee off?

As a single working mother, Josie wanted the best of both worlds for herself and her teenage daughter.

While the saying goes "Do well, now do good", a reverse of that would describe Josie aptly. Having graduated from a local university with an Economics degree, she had always harboured an ambition to serve the nation through a public service career. Her career stints at Changi Airport first, and later at LTA, helped her fulfil that ambition of doing good.

This mantra to "do good" had also extended into her private life. An advocate for energy conservation, she did more than talk about championing energy conservation — she walked the walk. Her home was fitted with energy-saving LED lights, and she took public transport to and from work and wherever she went. Once, in a bid to drive the message on the preciousness of water, she even rationed the water used at home over one weekend. She and Sarah had to be doubly careful with how the buckets of water were sparingly used throughout that weekend.

Having done all this good, Josie felt that age was catching up with her and thought that it's high time to focus on doing well in her career.

As a director of LTA's Corporate Planning & Development department, her job had been steady and rewarding. Her career had given her numerous opportunities to meet several high-flying personnel in the transportation sector – both government officials as well as industry captains. She enjoyed hobnobbing with the who's who.

But Josie desired more. She knew she was smart, that the corporate world suited her, and that she was a fighter.

These qualities augured well for her to climb higher. She was motivated, and had the ability to do well. What she needed now was the opportunity.

Golf Buddies

About once every fortnight, Josie would play a game of golf with two of her friends – Leo and EY – just to get away from corporate stress. When she first started golfing, she was perturbed by the amount of water used by the operators of golf courses. She had not known it was so costly to maintain a golf course.

Once, she had a night golf game. The amount of electricity needed to light the golf course for the cool evening game stunned her.

With her pro-Earth conservation attitude, these observations disturbed Josie.

But that took a turn when she soon realised that several senior honchos also played golf. Sometimes, she got to meet them and they ended up exchanging business cards and keeping in contact, widening her business contacts beyond the transportation sector.

"Perhaps it's time to do well and let 'do good' take a backseat," thought Josie, referring to her ambition to further her career.

While it had been merely her observation that many C-suite people played golf, a previous conversation with Leo, her golfing friend, set her thinking that perhaps there's more to golfing than just a social game.

At 6 am on a lazy Saturday, the group of three were at the first hole waiting for EY to take his swing. The occasional slight cool breeze gave a little lift to three heavy-eyed faces.

Leo mentioned that his brother-in-law, an Economics professor, had just completed a very novel research on golfing.

Excited at the relationship between golfing and economics, Josie, an Economics major, asked him what it was about.

In between strolls from one hole to the next, Leo slowly revealed the findings.

Women and Board Seats

Women's share of corporate director board seats varies tremendously across countries. While women are still far behind men in board representation, it appears that companies in Asia lag behind their non-Asian counterparts in welcoming on board women directors.

[I]n Asia, women's share of board seats is low and uneven, varying from 2.6 percent and 3.3 percent in Korea and Japan respectively, to 7.7 percent in Singapore, and 8.6 percent in India.

Women make up 26 percent of board directorship in the United Kingdom, 22 percent in Australia and 19 percent in the United States. But in Asia, women's share of board seats is low and uneven, varying from 2.6 percent and 3.3 percent in Korea and Japan respectively, to 7.7 percent in Singapore, and 8.6 percent in India.

Yet, studies have shown that companies with more than 10 percent of female board members enjoy, on average, higher returns on assets and equities than companies with less female representation.

A Boys' Game

"It's not surprising that gender affects climbing the corporate ladder. Historically, there has always been a glass ceiling," Leo remarked. "This starts from when we were young. Studies show that children recognise suitable gender-related activities and behaviours at an early age. Boys can climb trees and jump across sofas, but girls can't. I have a daughter and I don't want her to be stereotyped into what she can and cannot do because of her gender."

"Golf falls into this category," added EY. "Golf is seen as a boys' game. It's a male dominated game. The old boys' club, if you will. Josie, you are an exception."

Golf provides an invaluable social network, especially important in the corporate world. This social capital may influence career progress.

"But it goes beyond that. It's not just a boys' game. Golf provides an invaluable social network, especially important in the corporate world. This social capital may influence career progress," added Leo.

That last statement resonated with Josie. She had observed the socialisation among the golfers, and generally, these golfers were the industry captains or up-and-coming ones. She had always thought there was more than meets the eye behind what appeared to be no more than just a relaxing game of golf. It seemed that there was some social bonding going on that might open doors for career advancement.

"So what did your brother-in-law find?" asked a curious Josie. "We know golf is a men's game. So what does it mean for women playing golf?"

"A lot. Let's enjoy our golf for now. I'll fill you in at lunch," responded Leo.

The Research

Lunch at the Orchid Country Club was a buffet at the terrace café. Finding a corner for the three of them helped in the conversation amid the din from other golfers returning from their game.

"My brother-in-law teaches Economics at NUS. He's quite a golf fanatic himself and one day, while having his lunch, like what we're doing now, he noticed that there were only a handful of women playing golf. While that in itself is not surprising, he also noticed that he recognised most of these women — they were senior appointment holders," Leo elaborated. "That got my brother-in-law thinking. What separates these women from the other working women who are less successful in their career?"

In corporate Singapore, golf is an important social networking tool. But research shows that social networks often operate along gender lines. As such, golf being a male-dominated sport lends itself to reinforce social networks and bonding among men, potentially limiting its usefulness to female golf players.

[P]laying golf allows women to enter prominent social networks and increase their involvement in the labour market. By engaging in a predominantly male activity, women may gain additional social capital ...

However, one may argue that playing golf allows women to enter prominent social networks and increase their involvement in the labour market. By engaging in a predominantly male activity, women may gain additional social capital, even beyond that of male golfers. In other words, playing the boys' game may render female golfers being accepted by predominantly male corporate boards.

"My brother-in-law studied the directors of over 430 Singapore-based firms listed on the Singapore Stock Exchange over a 15-year period," Leo continued. "He also gathered data from the same period from golfers' handicap books, allowing them to match directors with their golfing statistics. From these two sources of information, he was able to generate a comprehensive database of over 10,000 golfers and 1,600 directors.

"First, he noticed that whether you are a director or not, there's no difference in your golf skills," Leo laughed.

"Haha . . . Then we can beat our bosses at golf," laughed EY.

While EY was more interested in satisfying his hunger pangs and was wolfing down his food, Josie was listening attentively. After all, this could influence her career.

[O]n average, females are 90 percent less likely to serve on the boards of directors.... Playing golf is associated with a stronger propensity to serve on corporate boards for women than for men by 54 percent. In other words, relative to the effect of male golfers, women who play golf are 74 percent more likely to serve on corporate boards.

"He found that almost nine in 10 of golfers are male. This is not surprising. Among the board of directors, 90.6 percent are male. Together, the odds ratio by gender and board membership stands at 0.094 for female. This means that on average, females are 90 percent less likely to serve on the boards of directors," said Leo.

"Nothing surprising," thought Josie.

"While this may not be all that surprising, does playing golf help break the gender glass ceiling in board representation? That was what my brother-in-law wanted to find out."

That got Josie's antennae-like ears up again.

"He found that golfers have a higher probability of holding a directorship with an odds ratio of 59.9. However, when comparing the odds ratio by gender, playing golf helps women more than men. Playing golf is associated with a stronger propensity to serve on corporate boards for women than for men by 54 percent. In other words, relative to the effect of male golfers, women who play golf are 74 percent more likely to serve on corporate boards."

"Josie, that's you! You are 74 percent more likely to be a board director than us!" chuckled EY, who suddenly seemed more interested in the study than his food.

"*Siao* (meaning 'crazy'). Just listen," Josie retorted, trying to brush off that she might one day be on a corporate board. Although deep down, she was somewhat pleased and excited. She tried hard not to smile. She was, what some might say, passively aggressive.

"Interestingly, my brother-in-law said that this was particularly more evident among firms with larger market capitalisation than those with smaller one. For small firms, golfing did not affect female board membership. Instead, female golfers in large firms are 125 percent more likely to serve on a board relative to male golfers in similar sized firms," Leo continued.

"There you go! Josie again — LTA is a large firm. You can be on the board," kidded EY.

"Please lah. LTA is not a publicly-listed company," Josie poked fun at her friend's mistake.

EY wasn't bothered. The fact still remained that as a golf player, Josie had a higher chance of being a board member than other non-golfing women. "Eh, Leo. We are in good company. We'll have a female board member soon in our golfing gang. Josie, you must not forget us when you become a board member. You cannot be *atas* and neglect us, ok?"

Josie rolled her eyes.

"So what has that got to do with social capital?" asked Josie, who was still pondering on the commonality between golfing and economics.

"Well, this gives some evidence of social capital at work," explained Leo. "I'm not that familiar with the study but I'll try my best to explain. This was what my brother-in-law said — Larger firms are presumably more hierarchical. There are so many layers to climb before you reach the top. So to be able to get on the board despite the hierarchy suggests social capital is at play. And golfing helps women more than men to get to this board leadership.

"My brother-in-law also said something about how this finding varies by industry. Industries with low female representation have prohibitive barriers to networking. But if such industries have a higher female board representation relative to high-female-representation industries, and these female board members are golf players, then my brother-in-law said this is suggestive that social capital is present.

"And he found exactly that. Women are more likely to serve on the board of directors in low-female-representation industries (by 117 percent) if they play golf, relative to men."

"Fascinating," thought Josie.

To her, the study highlighted two issues important for her career ambition. First, although there was a gender glass ceiling she had to cross, there were means to overcome the gender disparity. She should engage in social activities that ran counter to social norms or behaviours because these activities somewhat mitigated the glass ceiling in corporate boards.

Second, social capital and networking could foster career outcomes. The study was implying to Josie that she could enhance her chances of serving on a board of a large listed company if she would involve herself in male-dominated social activities such as golf. That was what she planned to do in the years to come.

WANT TO KNOW MORE?

This chapter is based on Sumit Agarwal, Qian Wenlan, David M. Reeb and Sing Tien Foo, "Golf Buddies and Board Diversity," (12 December 2015). Available at SSRN: https://ssrn.com/abstract=2702742 or http://dx.doi.org/10.2139/ssrn.2702742

Other materials came from *Building Diversity in Asia Pacific Boardrooms*, Korn Ferry Diversity Scorecard 2016, Centre for Governance, Institutions and Organisations, National University of Singapore Business School.

CHAPTER 13

Papa, Don't Forget to Switch off the Lights

"Good morning, girls," said Mrs Johan at the school's assembly. Mrs Johan was the teacher involved in pastoral care in Sarah's secondary school.

"Later this afternoon at 3 pm, the upper secondary level girls are to attend the talk we have specially organised with NEA, the National Environment Agency, on energy conservation."

"Boring . . .," said Sarah to her friend. She had more than enough of such talks from her pro-conservation mum.

"Sarah, turn off your tap when brushing your teeth. Sarah, why is the toilet light left switched on? Sarah, leave the door closed when you switch on the air-conditioning. Think about how much you are wasting." These were the repetitive admonishments Sarah received whenever her mother paid extra attention to what she was up to.

"And now, I've got to hear the same thing again in school," she sighed. She had considered skipping the talk. Her piano teacher would be coming that evening and Sarah wanted to practise her piece first.

But Mrs Johan had eagle's eyes. She would know if Sarah gave the talk a miss. And because Mrs Johan and her mother went a long way back – they had known each other since their days in primary school – it was likely that Mrs Johan would inform her mum if Sarah skipped the talk. That would spell trouble with a capital T.

"Well, I'd rather be bored than be scolded," thought Sarah, relenting after weighing her options.

Besides, Mrs Johan did say the talk might be helpful for her English 'O' levels. "You must always be prepared for whatever topic that may come up in your orals or essays. So, be widely read. Knowledge is power and will not hold anyone back."

Sarah hoped Mrs Johan was right.

NEA

Mr Leong from NEA was a tall lanky man. Standing 1.9 metres tall, he hunched a little as he swaggered to the podium to give the talk.

Nervously, he tapped twice on the microphone producing a "tud, tud" sound. "Eh . . . Testing, testing."

"Grr . . . Why do people always tap on the mike before they speak?" hissed an irritable Sarah. "Just speak. If the mike isn't working, you'll know!" Her patience was wearing thin. A long day's worth of lessons had tired her out. This was worsened by Singapore's sauna-like weather; the high-20s to mid-30s temperature coupled with high humidity seeped energy out of her. Yet, she was had to stay on for the talk.

"Good afternoon," greeted Mr Leong. "On behalf of NEA, thank you for inviting me to give a talk on energy conservation.

"You probably have heard of the numerous ways to save energy – don't set your air-conditioning temperature to below 25°C, don't keep your refrigerator fully packed with food, switch off your iron just before you finish pressing the last piece of clothing – blah blah blah. Going through these will be an insult to your intelligence. You are smart young ladies. Instead, for today, I'm going to present you with a novel and yet effective way to get people to adopt more energy efficient practices.

"While you may say that many of such ways of energy conservation are common sense, this method that I'm going to discuss is so common that it is right under our noses. Yet, we have often taken it for granted and never used it to the fullest extent as a means to conserve energy."

Sarah was intrigued. "What is this man talking about?" she wondered.

"By way of showing your hands, how many of you have been told by any of your parents, either mum or dad, not to forget to switch off the lights?" asked Mr Leong.

He paused and waited for hands to be raised.

"Haha . . . Almost all of you. Again by show of hands, how many of you have been told not to leave the TV on when nobody is watching?" Mr Leong continued.

Half of the audience raised their hands.

"Now, what if I say that you could say the same thing to your parents? That you could say, 'Papa, don't forget to switch off the lights when you leave the bathroom.' How many of you would just love to turn the table and say that to your parents?"

Everyone laughed. Of course, who wouldn't want a role reversal?

Satisfied that he had gotten the audience's attention, Mr Leong began on what he had intended to share for the talk: Project Carbon Zero.

Project Carbon Zero

NEA partnered with the Singapore Environment Council (SEC) to organise an energy-saving competition known as 'Project Carbon Zero' for primary and secondary schools. The competition sets a goal for students to reduce overall electricity usage at home.

[S]tudents are ... expected to bring ... energy-saving messages home and nudge their family members to do their part in reducing electricity usage.

In the participating schools, teachers in science and social studies classes would educate students on the importance of energy conservation, and share with them specific energy-saving tips and advice. For instance, students are advised not to leave appliances on standby mode, and to set their air-conditioners at 25°C to save energy at home. They are also expected to bring these energy-saving messages home and nudge their family members to do their part in reducing electricity usage.

To participate in the competition, students are required to bring their monthly household electricity bills to school for verification and tracking purposes for eight months — four months prior to the start of the competition and four months during the competition period.

This corresponds to electricity bills from January to April before the commencement of the competition and from May to August when the competition is in progress.

The difference in total electricity consumption between these two periods is then computed. Over 290 students from 30 schools participated.

The Policy Experiment

"While this is a competition to promote energy conservation, it is also a policy experiment," Mr Leong said. "A policy experiment means that a study is conducted so that the results can be used to make policy decisions.

"In this instance, although we ran a student competition to encourage households to use less energy, we could also use the information to test whether encouraging school children to follow energy-saving tips and influence their family members to do likewise can result in less energy consumption."

"Grr . . . Policy experiment . . . Boring," Sarah grumbled under her breath.

"Now, when people influence others, how is the behaviour like?" asked Mr Leong. Hearing no response from the audience, he explained, "You interact with your neighbours, you meet your friends downstairs at the void deck, you meet the uncle at the coffee shop . . . And you may indirectly impact energy savings to them because you've been asked to help spread this message. You may just casually say 'don't leave your appliances on standby mode after using'. These are what we call 'nudges'.

"But as school children, your influence is likely to be limited. The nudging effects are likely to be stronger in neighbourhoods located close to the participating schools than in neighbourhoods away from these schools.

"For instance, if you live and go to school in Toa Payoh, I don't think you will be able to influence residents living in Tampines.

"So, how do we know who is who? Who lives near a participating school?"

Mr Leong paused for a while to see whether anyone volunteered a guess.

"As you know well, MOE (Ministry of Education) has a distance-based policy that gives priority in school allocation to students living within a two-kilometre radius from a school. Parents generally prefer to enrol their children in schools that are close to their homes.

"Therefore, we used the home–school distance to define the areas where the energy-saving message from schoolchildren was likely to have the most direct impact on families. For simplicity, we say there was an intervention — an intervention in getting people to save energy and use less electricity.

"We used the two-kilometre home–school distance to identify the housing blocks that were likely to have students involved in the energy-saving competition. For these blocks, there was an intervention. Housing blocks outside the two-kilometre school zone were considered as not receiving the energy-saving message, henceforth no intervention.

"At the same time, we had the monthly electricity consumption data for over 6,600 HDB and private housing blocks from January to December for the year that Project Carbon Zero was launched, giving us over 69,000 utility data for each block for each month. We identified those that were located within the school zone where the energy-saving campaign message was given and those outside the zone where residents were less likely to have heard of the campaign."

As Mr Leong was going through the details of how the experiment was conducted, Sarah was telling herself, "This is so systematic. Boring as it may seem, a study has to be properly carried out to obtain true findings. This is what my friends and I should be doing for our Social

Studies project. We need to study the 'before' and 'after'. I hope my friends are listening to Mr Leong and getting ideas for our project."

Campaign Effects

Mr Leong began reeling out the findings.

"We found that the lowest average monthly energy consumption is in February and the highest average energy consumption is in June. Household electricity consumption is generally lower in the first four months of the year from January to April, compared to the months of May to August. Understandably so, as May to August are the hottest months in Singapore, and thus families are likely to switch on their air-conditioning more frequently."

Mr Leong waited for a response. Then, he continued, "I hope you are not falling asleep because I'm coming to the interesting part of the findings.

"If you take a look at this graph. It shows two consumption patterns. The dashed line is electricity consumption by blocks near the schools where students took part in the energy-saving competition. So there had been intervention for this group of households. The solid line is electricity consumption by blocks outside the two-kilometre demarcation from the school zone. So, it is unlikely that these

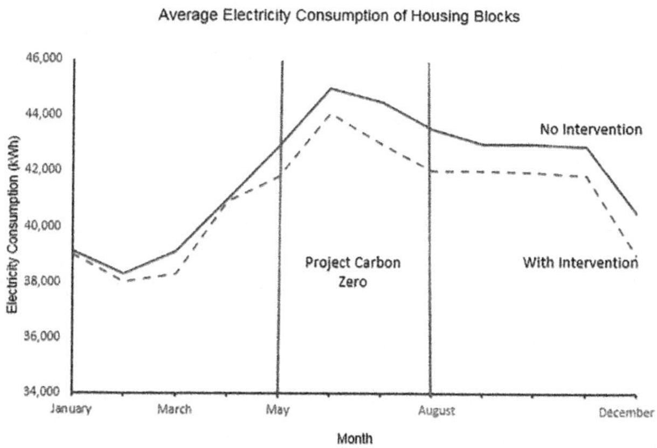

households would have been exposed to students who had taken part in Project Carbon Zero, resulting in no intervention."

Mr Leong showed a Powerpoint slide displaying the results.

"You see two vertical lines which represent May to August when Project Carbon Zero was on.

"While before May — January to April — there was no significant differences in electricity consumption between households that were exposed to children who had taken part in the energy-conservation competition and households that were less likely to be exposed to such children, this was not the pattern from May onwards.

"Can you see how the gap between the solid and dashed lines start to get bigger especially from June onwards when Project Carbon Zero was in full swing? That means the campaign was beginning to take effect. People were changing their behaviour in how they used their electrical appliances."

There was a soft chorus of "ahhs" from the students. Some had their finger pointing in the air at the chart, while discussing with their friends.

"Overall, we found that during the campaign period of May to August, households with the intervention used 1.8 percent less electricity than households without the intervention. So the campaign to use less electricity worked. School children, by gently persuading their parents and their neighbours to save energy, influenced them to use less as reflected by the smaller utilities bills that the intervened households had to pay.

School children, by gently persuading their parents and their neighbours to save energy, influenced them to use less as reflected by the smaller utilities bills that the intervened households had to pay.

"It turned out there was a difference between primary and secondary schoolchildren. Now, who do you think did a better job in influencing their parents – primary or secondary school students?" asked Mr Leong.

"Secondary," shouted someone from the audience. Everyone laughed because they were from a secondary school.

"Sorry lah. The primary school students outdid you. Households in apartments near the participating primary schools used 2.1 percent less electricity than those near the participating secondary schools," said Mr Leong as he dampened their overconfidence.

Households in apartments near the participating primary schools used 2.1 percent less electricity than those near the participating secondary schools.

"For households near participating secondary schools, the campaign was also effective but to a smaller degree. They used 1.5 percent less electricity than households living more than two kilometres away from participating secondary schools."

Sarah's mind began to absorb the information. She knew the importance of saving electricity to her mum. Mum would be keen on these findings.

"Wait . . . Don't get too excited. I saved the best for last," said Mr Leong as he tried to make himself heard. He knew the students were getting restless. It had been a long day. Moreover, the students probably would have to go home for their private tuition classes as the exams were just round the corner. So he hurriedly summarised the last bit of findings.

"Now, we know that the campaign worked. Just getting children to talk to their parents and neighbours about saving energy can change behaviour resulting in less energy used.

"But importantly, did such savings persist? If it doesn't, then what's the point? After all, we can't be doing such campaigns all the time."

All the girls nodded. They understood the value of sustainability.

"And I can read some of your minds. Some of you are thinking, 'Of course lah. You got this improved behaviour because the campaign was on. It's only temporary. When the campaign is over, it's back to square one for everybody.' Am I right?" asked Mr Leong.

Some girls chuckled because indeed, some of them were cynical that such nudging would simply do the trick of changing behaviour.

Mr Leong relished as he continued with the findings.

"It turned out that after the campaign was over in August, that behaviour of using less electricity persisted, though not to the extent as when the campaign was on full steam. It persisted enough not to go back to the higher levels of electricity consumption before the campaign.

[A]fter the campaign was over ... that behaviour of using less electricity ... persisted enough not to go back to the higher levels of electricity consumption before the campaign.

"In fact, on average, households with the campaign intervention saved about 1.6 percent in their monthly electricity bills way after Project Carbon Zero was over."

Sarah's mind was racing. While the amount might not be much on a per household basis, it could come to a princely sum when aggregated across all households. She knew she had to think on a macro scale and not just focus on her own household.

She was also amazed that such savings came from mere gentle coaxing from schoolchildren to their parents and neighbours. What more if there were other campaigns to encourage energy conservation? Or similar campaigns that encouraged people to care for the environment?

"Maybe if I tell Professor Sing's daughter how to save energy, she'll be able to persuade her mum and dad. And I'll work on cute Ethan, the little boy next door. Once he grows a little older, maybe he can also influence Uncle Teng and Auntie Siew Ling to save electricity," Sarah mused. "Hmm . . . I'll start my own Project Sarah," thought Sarah, smiling to herself.

But for now, she had two important things she needed to do – that was to tell her mum about the findings, and figure out how this information could be used should a question on energy conservation come up for her exams.

WANT TO KNOW MORE?

This chapter is based on Sumit Agarwal, Satyanarain Rengarajan and Sing Tien Foo, "Nudges by School Children and Electricity Conservation: Evidence from the 'Project Carbon Zero' Campaign in Singapore," *Energy Economics*, (forthcoming). Available at SSRN: https://ssrn.com/abstract=2529183 or http://dx.doi.org/10.2139/ssrn.2529183; and Sumit Agarwal and Sing Tien Foo, "Empowering Kids Key to Saving Electricity," *The New Paper*, (21 August 2017). http://www.tnp.sg/news/views/empowering-kids-key-saving-electricity

CHAPTER 14

Mama, Don't Forget to Switch on the Air-con

When Teng and Siew Ling first visited the Serangoon flat while house hunting, they had noticed an ongoing construction project for a new community centre at the plot of land next to the flat. At that time, the construction had only just started and there was not much of a cacophony during the day.

The building of this community centre was necessary to cater to the growing number of elderly residents whose recreational needs had changed. Besides having seminar rooms for classes targeted at upgrading the skills of younger residents, the centre would also house more rooms for the ageing residents including a gym with elder-friendly exercise equipment.

That was a selling point. With Ma and Pa living with them, the proximity to the community centre would give the old folks an opportunity to hang around with neighbours and engage in low-impact exercises.

But before that could happen, they would have to put up with the incessant hammering coming from the construction works. The foundation was being laid and tons of steel rods and sand were piled on one side. While generally tolerable, the din was at times deafening.

Air-con or Not?

"Today was a bad day," Ma complained to Teng when he got home at 5 pm for a short dinner before heading out to find more passengers again. Teng had switched to having the taxi all to himself, with no co-driver. "The weather is so hot and the noise next door is just too deafening," referring to the ongoing construction works.

"Yeah. Singapore's weather is getting hotter and hotter. It's the global warming thing," was Teng's tired response.

"At least you've got air-con in your taxi. We don't," complained Ma again, seeming to insinuate that Teng's taxi driving was far more comfortable and less challenging than staying at home to keep an eye on Ethan. "And Ethan was not co-operative today. He didn't have his afternoon nap because of the construction noise. He ended up feeling super cranky. This cannot, that cannot — He was crying and crying the whole afternoon. It was like a competition to see who's louder. The construction or Ethan. All these are giving me a splitting headache."

"Eh, Teng. The noise is driving me crazy too, not to mention your mother's non-stop complaining. It's like sense-surround sound, inside outside also have noise," Pa interjected with light humour.

Ma's grumblings went on and on, even when Siew Ling came back.

Like a malfunctioned recording, the same message was being played over and over again. Ma continued to bring up her grouses with

Singapore's scorching heat and Ethan's non-stop crying induced by the construction noise.

"Ma, then close the windows and switch on the air-con," offered Siew Ling, just to keep peace at home.

"Aiyah! That will be so expensive. It's such a waste of money," said Ma as she frowned at Siew Ling's lack of financial discipline over spending. "You spent a bomb buying this big flat. And now you still want to spend more money? You should be saving. Air-conditioning is too expensive."

"Gosh," thought Siew Ling. "Putting up with the construction noise is not desirable, but neither is switching on the air-con. There's no way we can please this old lady. Maybe that's what I'll become when I get older – we become difficult to please."

An Expensive Alternative

But what her mother-in-law had said about air-conditioning being expensive is true.

As a hot and humid country located 1° north of the Equator, Singaporean households use the bulk of electricity for ventilation and cooling purposes. Those living in HDB flats consume about 370 kilowatt hour of electricity each month, half the amount consumed by households living in private properties.

Air-conditioners and refrigeration appliances account for nearly two-thirds of the household electricity bills. The NEA estimates that the amount of energy used by fans is only one-tenth of an air-conditioner. But fans alone may not be sufficient to ward off the country's enervating heat.

In Singapore, the air-conditioner consumes the largest amount of electricity in an average household. More than one-third (37 percent) of a typical household's electricity bill comes from the use of air-conditioning.

In Singapore, the air-conditioner consumes the largest amount of electricity in an average household. More than one-third (37 percent) of a typical household's electricity bill comes from the use of air-conditioning.

Like many densely-built tropical cities, Singapore experiences a climatic phenomenon known as urban heat island (UHI) effects. UHI effects in Singapore cause temperatures to vary up to 7°C between the morning and the evening hours, and by 4°C between the urban and the non-urban vegetated areas.

UHI effects are more severe in housing estates located near construction sites where noise and air pollutions generated by construction activities deterioriate the quality of the indoor living environment.

UHI effects are more severe in housing estates located near construction sites where noise and air pollutions generated by construction activities deteriorate the quality of the indoor living environment.

Having several construction projects occurring concurrently in Singapore worsens these UHI effects.

When households close their windows to keep the noise and heat out from their homes, they end up using more fans and air-conditioners. By changing the ventilation strategy, they incur higher costs for comfort, which is reflected in rising electricity bills.

"It's ok Ma. If the noise gets unbearable, you, Pa and Ethan can stay in your bedroom, close the windows and switch on the air-conditioning," said Siew Ling again. "You have the TV in your room, right? You can watch TV together. As all of you are in the same room, we won't be using too much air-con too. So switching on the air-conditioner is not so wasteful.

"And you don't have to switch on the air-con all the time. We have the 'Save' mode where the air-con starts automatically only when the temperature rises.

"And if you put the temperature at 26°C, that will help cut down on the air-con bill too."

"Grr . . . That's easy to say now. Wait until you see your electricity bill. It's so wasteful. Electricity is so expensive," Ma continued grumbling. "When I was young, we would *tahan.*"

"With all that complaining, I wouldn't have guessed that she was *tahan-ing*. Well, it's up to her. I've given her an alternative," thought Siew Ling, knowing that it's not easy living together with in-laws.

Teng came back again at 9 pm after a short evening plying the roads for passengers. The TV set was switched on with nobody really watching. Ma and Pa were dozing off, as was usual when they were watching TV in the evenings. A news item about Singaporeans using more electricity flashed across the screen, but neither Teng nor Siew Ling quite got the content as they were pre-occupied with looking after Ethan.

"I'll check tomorrow's newspapers. Maybe that will help us make a decision as to whether to use our air-conditioning in the day or not," thought Teng.

The News

The news report that they missed was on household electricity consumption. It reported that a quasi-experiment had been conducted to test whether construction works could affect household electricity consumption.

A quasi-experiment is a study where there are naturally formed groups that demonstrate different behaviours arising from certain characteristics in which the groups differ.

In the reported news, there were two clusters of HDB blocks that differed in terms of whether there were ongoing construction works near the blocks. HDB households in blocks within one kilometre of an active construction site were identified as one group and those not affected by construction activities as another group. Their respective utility bills were monitored to see whether they differed in electricity consumption during the period of construction.

The aim of the quasi-experiment was to address two questions:

(1) Do households change their 'ventilation strategy' by consuming more electricity via closing windows and turning on their air-conditioner for their indoor spaces in response to noise pollution from nearby construction activities?

(2) Does the increased use of electricity consumption of affected residents remain the same after the construction period is over?

The newspapers reported that the results showed construction activities increased electricity consumption of HDB households by 7.7 to 8.3 percent relative to those who lived outside one kilometre from the nearest construction site. Households that lived within one kilometre from large construction sites consumed more electricity in the same month of the year.

[C]onstruction activities increased electricity consumption of HDB households by 7.7 to 8.3 percent relative to those who lived outside one kilometre from the nearest construction site.

Billing for electricity use included a tariff of 0.27 cents per kilowatt hour. This translated to construction sites inducing each HDB block to spend almost $10,000 more annually by changing households' 'ventilation strategies'.

But more importantly, this behavioural change of turning on the air-conditioning appeared to be a permanent shift in electricity consumption behaviour.

After the construction was over, households of those blocks affected by the construction did not completely adjust their electricity consumption back to the levels prior to the construction period.

After the construction was over, households of those blocks affected by the construction did not completely adjust their electricity consumption back to the levels prior to the construction period. Even though they were no longer affected by construction activities, they continued to use their air-conditioning and fans almost the same way as during the construction period.

Reflections

After reading the news report, Teng was somewhat hesitant to encourage his parents to close the windows and use the air-conditioning. What if they became so accustomed to and spoilt with the comfort provided by the air-conditioning that they continued to use the air-conditioning on a regular basis even after the construction was over? Getting Ma to stop using air-conditioning would probably lead to another earful of complaints. Then, Teng would curse himself for even suggesting it to them.

With him and Siew Ling away for work, they could not monitor the usage of air-conditioning.

"I wonder whether Josie has read this," as Teng thought of his environmentally-conscious neighbour. "Would she resort to using fans rather than air-conditioning? Or maybe she'll just stay out more often to avoid the noise. Luckily she's working and doesn't have to suffer much in the day from the construction."

When Siew Ling returned home that evening, Teng discussed the situation with her.

"I don't think you have a choice, dear," said Siew Ling. "She's your mother. She and Pa are living with us to help look after Ethan. They are doing us a favour. And how many more years do you think they have? We should make their lives as comfortable as possible."

Then, pausing for quite a while, she continued, "Maybe, the building authorities should be like *mata* (meaning 'policeman') and check that construction sites do not become nuisance to the public. I know we have regulations on noise levels. But it looks like it may not be sufficient.

"It also means these construction works should be completed as quickly as possible. We don't want people to get used to living with the air-con switched on. The longer the construction is on, the more difficult it would be to kick this habit when the construction is over.

"For each block to spend an extra $10,000 each year to close windows and switch on the air-con is a lot when we add up the number of affected blocks. I think the government should consider tougher requirements. Maybe the opposition parties will bring this up as an election issue?" Siew Ling winked.

Teng added, "And how about other expenses? The newspapers only reported electricity usage. How about hearing problems from the loud noise? We don't know the long-term effects of such construction sites. Some people may even turn their TV sets up louder just to beat the noise. Then the whole neighbourhood will be even noisier.

"Siew Ling, do you think other kinds of noise will also lead to more air-con being used? Whenever I drive along expressways and pass houses facing the highways or main roads, I always wonder whether their living environment is noisy.

"Or those near MRT tracks, I bet their surroundings are noisier. Just like where we used to live near the KTM Railway track. Do you think those houses use more electricity too?

"Moreover, such noises are more permanent — unlike construction noise which you know it will end when the project is completed — the noises generated by vehicles seem to be a long-term problem for people living next to expressways and MRT lines. Does that mean more electricity is used all the time? Or do people get used to the noise and somehow adapt to it without having to close their windows?"

Amused by Teng's flood of questions, his wife replied with a smile, "I don't know — but I think your primary school teacher would be so proud that you're asking such questions now."

WANT TO KNOW MORE?

This chapter is based on Sumit Agarwal, Satyanarain Rengarajan, Sing Tien Foo and Derek Vollmer, "Effects of Construction Activities on Residential Electricity Consumption: Evidence from Singapore's Public Housing Estates," (24 November 2015). Available at SSRN: https://ssrn.com/abstract=2371314 or http://dx.doi.org/10.2139/ssrn.2371314

CHAPTER 15

Boy Boy, Go to a Good School

Teng and Siew Ling had been living in their new flat for almost two years. The construction of the community centre was finally completed.

Ma and Pa had been kind enough to uproot and give up their independence as well as the comfort of their old neighbourhood to move in with them. The grandparents certainly loved being close to their grandchild. Ethan, as boisterous as any toddler would be, enjoyed his doting grandparents – sometimes a little too much for Siew Ling's liking.

Siew Ling had enrolled Ethan for music appreciation lessons. She heard from her friends on the importance of stimulating both the left and right sides of a child's brain. To ensure that Ethan was not all cerebral with no brawn, she and Teng had brought him to the community swimming pool to develop a sense of co-ordination and agility.

As for pre-primary education, it was fairly easy to register Ethan in a nursery near their Serangoon home. There were plenty to choose from.

Friends had also passed on several second-hand books from their older kids. "Quite *sayang* (meaning 'wasteful') to just throw them away," they had said. Indeed so. They were board books in English – some that Siew Ling had never heard of – like Eric Carle's *The Very Hungry Caterpillar* and Margaret Wise Brown's *Goodnight Moon*. Ethan enjoyed listening to these books as his parents tried to read to him in the most expressive English they could put together – especially when Teng pretended to be the hungry caterpillar or when Ethan and his parents tried finding the little mouse together in *Goodnight Moon*.

Siew Ling also augmented her son's mini library with several colourful children's books with big prints bought from Popular Bookstore. As she was more comfortable with Mandarin, she had bought quite a number of Chinese books to ensure that Ethan would be effectively bilingual.

But what could potentially be a cause for academic anxiety was where to place Ethan for his primary education.

Initially, Teng had wanted Ethan to go to Fairfield Methodist School. But having bought a flat in Serangoon and not along Dover Road where the school is situated, that wish had been put to paid.

There were several primary schools in the vicinity including St. Gabriel's and a newly opened Yangzheng Primary School.

Siew Ling and Teng wondered what services they had to render to these schools to get Ethan in – should they offer to serve as road-crossing wardens, or librarians? After all, they wanted the best for their precious only child.

Like typical *kiasu* parents, they wanted to be absolutely well-prepared so that they would not lag behind in getting the choice school for

Ethan. Though he was only three years old, his parents felt it was never too early to start paving the way to ensure that Ethan would get into a good school. If it meant Siew Ling or Teng doing voluntary school services, so be it.

The Two-Kilometre Rule

In Singapore, the Ministry of Education has a ruling where priority in enrolling one's child into a school goes to households with addresses within two kilometres of the school, and those within one kilometre have an edge over those between one to two kilometres. This ruling makes practical sense as it reduces the time spent on house–school transportation.

Even though Teng and Siew Ling enjoyed the two-kilometre zone advantage to some schools, competition was still stiff, as the HDB blocks were chock-a-block with many school-going children. There could even be more eligible Primary 1 children than available vacancies.

But that was one of Peter's selling points about the Serangoon flat – its location near choice schools.

It is a commonly known fact that houses near choice schools tend to be more expensive than houses located further away.

Singaporeans have, for a long time, been purchasing or renting properties nearby to choice schools, preferably within one kilometre of the aforementioned schools, at least a year before registering their child for Primary 1 education so as to enjoy registration priority for their child to be in one of these schools. This has ramped up demand for both the sale and rental markets in these locations.

Every School Is a Good School

Teng and Siew Ling remembered listening to the Prime Minister's National Day Rally speech some years back that had coincidentally addressed the very topic that they had been anxious about. The Prime Minister had acknowledged the deeply rooted rent-seeking behaviour of parents:

> ". . . within the same housing estate, two separate schools, few hundred metres apart, parents will go to great lengths to bring their children into School A (popular school) instead of School B. . . . Having got a place in a good school, they want a place in another school which in their view will be better for their kid. Sometimes, they succeed, sometimes they do not. But the belief is very deep."

In his speech, he alluded to the story of Mencius, a famous Chinese philosopher and principal interpreter of Confucianism, whose mother moved three times before she found the right neighbourhood, next to a school to raise her son.

The Prime Minister cited a local mother (more aggressive than Mencius' mother) who moved not three but four times within Singapore just to increase the chances of getting her eldest child into a good primary school.

Clearly, the one-kilometre and one-to-two-kilometre priority rules have driven housing mobility by parents who want to live close to choice schools to gain the priority advantage. These parents have a view that certain schools are better than others, and they want the better school for their child.

[T]he one-kilometre and one-to-two-kilometre priority rules have driven housing mobility by parents who want to live close to choice schools to gain the priority advantage.

The Prime Minister acknowledged this perspective:

> "There are two different perspectives on education, on schools in Singapore. One is the MOE (Ministry of Education) perspective – 'every school is a good school' . . . [W]e give every school the teachers, the resources, the backing. We help many of our schools develop niches of excellence. We make sure that the whole system is of a high standard . . . But parents and students have a different perspective. They accept the MOE argument but they still have strong preferences for certain schools."

What Peter Said

"I wonder how this will affect our property price," Siew Ling thought.

"Hey, dear, do you remember what Peter told us when we were house hunting?" Siew Ling asked Teng. "Peter had said that our unit is good because it is close to some choice schools. And Nanyang Junior College is not too far off."

"Yup, I remember," replied Teng.

"And he mentioned something about a study on good schools. Do you remember what he said?" asked Siew Ling who was trying to remember what Peter had said and relate it to the National Day Rally speech.

"You are so forgetful," Teng chided his wife jokingly. "I'll try to explain in my best Peter impersonation. Remember, his English is now so good and polished.

"If I remember correctly, Peter said that there was a real estate study that identified houses located within the two priority zones of one kilometre and one to two kilometres, as well as houses in the two-to-four kilometre boundary. The researchers wanted to study whether relocation of a school will affect property prices. They used statistics from MOE to identify 16 schools that were relocated during a 10-year period, during which time they also collected housing transaction data for that same period. Public housing data were obtained from the HDB database, while private housing data were obtained from the Urban Redevelopment Authority.

"If I remember correctly, I think one of the schools relocated was your primary school – Haig Girls' School. It used to be at Jalan Tembusu, right? It moved to Koon Seng Road."

"Huh? I didn't know that. When did it move? Kind of lost part of its heritage, don't you think? That courtyard where we raised the flag every morning . . . I remember how I used to peek at the secondary school boys from Tanjong Katong Tech walking by. How come these schools move and move?" said Siew Ling nostalgically.

"That's life. Must move on," laughed Teng as he used his own 'move' pun.

"Anyway, back to Peter. I remember Peter drew these circles to show the locations of School A, School B and a house. Something like this.

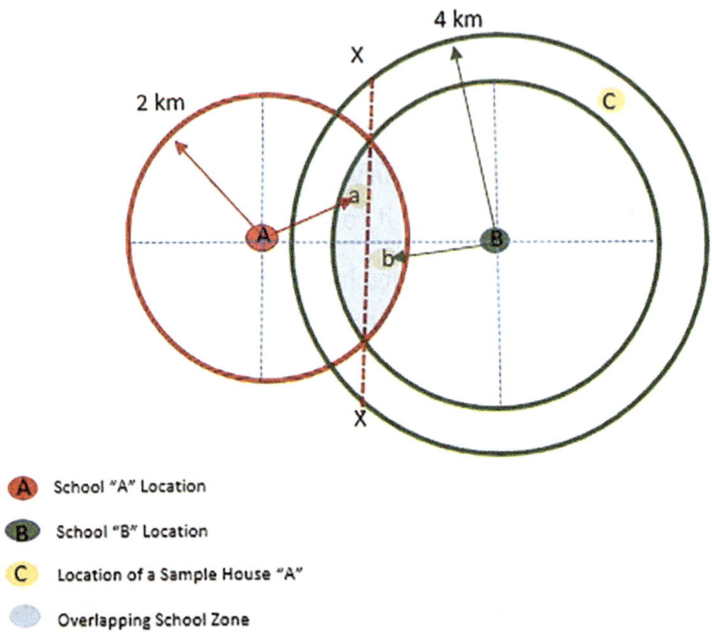

"I think Peter also said that the X–X vertical line cutting the overlapping zone splits the houses into two groups. For instance, the home–school distance of house 'a' which falls within the two-kilometre school zones of both Schools A and B is measured with reference to School A because School A is nearer. The distances of houses 'b' and 'c' are measured with reference to School B. Hence, within a two-kilometre boundary zone, it can be subdivided into non-overlapping zones and overlapping zones."

"Wow! Your memory is good, Teng. I only vaguely recall," said Siew Ling. "How come you remember these things but not my birthday?"

"Haha . . . I *chose* not to remember your birthday!" said Teng jokingly. "No lah. This one concerns money and so I thought I'd better remember, especially if I want to counter the cohort size effect of being born in the year of the Dragon. To this day, I still remember what my teacher told Peter and me about the cohort size effect. That was when I was in primary school. It was pretty traumatic for me to know that I may not do well in life, all because of being a Dragon baby."

"You are good. Financial success is not everything. Heart is more important," reassured Siew Ling. "Now, refresh me on the findings please."

"Peter said that they had collected a lot of data," Teng began to share. "If I'm not mistaken, I think they studied over 130,000 transactions of private non-landed houses and public HDB resale houses. The private houses were newer at five years old while the HDB flats were older at 23 years old.

"They also measured the distance of these houses to the closest schools. Most of these 16 schools relocated in December or January so as not to affect the school term," said Teng.

"Let me check my iPhone for details. I remember I'd photographed Peter's notes on transacted prices. There were so many. Wait ah," Teng paused as he went to the 'Photos' icon on his iPhone and scrolled. "Here it is. Ahh . . . These are the Singapore schools that relocated.

1	Haig Girls' School
2	Temasek Primary School
3	Convent of the Holy Infant Jesus Our Lady of the Nativity
4	Tech Whye Primary School
5	Si Ling Primary School
6	River Valley Primary School
7	Anglo-Chinese School (Junior)
8	Fuchun Primary School
9	Bukit Timah Primary School
10	Blangah Rise Primary School
11	Poi Ching Primary School
12	Raffles Girls' Primary School
13	Nan Chiau Primary School
14	Woodlands Primary School
15	Mee Toh Primary School
16	Mayflower Primary School

"My 'Photos' shows these numbers:

Averages	**Private Housing**	**HDB**
Selling price	$867,481	$251,232
Floor area	128 sq metres	96 sq metres
Age	5 years	23 years
Distance to old school location	3 km	3.8 km

Old School Location	**Less than 2-km**	**2 to 4 km**
Average distance to school	1.3 km	3 km
Average selling price	$525,880	$450,435

New School Location	**Less than 2-km**	**2 to 4 km**
Average distance to school	1.2 km	3 km
Average selling price	$491,259	$458,481

"Peter said that houses located within one kilometre from the school were sold at a 2.4 percent premium, and those located between one to two kilometres from the school were sold at a huge 17.5 percent premium compared to houses located between two to four kilometres from the school."

[H]ouses located within one kilometre from the school were sold at a 2.4 percent premium, and those located between one to two kilometres from the school were sold at a huge 17.5 percent premium compared to houses located between two to four kilometres from the school.

"Huh? Wait a minute. How come houses nearer the school do not command a higher premium than those located two kilometres away?" asked a puzzled Siew Ling.

"Yah, strange hor?" Teng agreed. He scratched his head and tried hard to recall what Peter had said. "Ahh . . . I remember. Peter said people complained about having traffic jam and noise if they live too near a school.

"I know this. Every morning between 6:45 to 7:30 am, I avoid the Dunearn–Bukit Timah Road area. There's a massive congestion because of Nanyang Primary School on one side, and Raffles Girls' Primary School, Singapore Chinese Girls' School and then Anglo-Chinese School on the other side. And the number of traffic lights in the area is crazy. I understand the traffic needs to be regulated but sometimes, I think this causes more jams instead.

"Let me google to see if I can find something about traffic lights in Singapore," said Teng as he searched his phone again. "Here we go.

"The dots are the traffic lights. See the whole bunch of dots at the bottom of Singapore? That area also has lots of congestion.

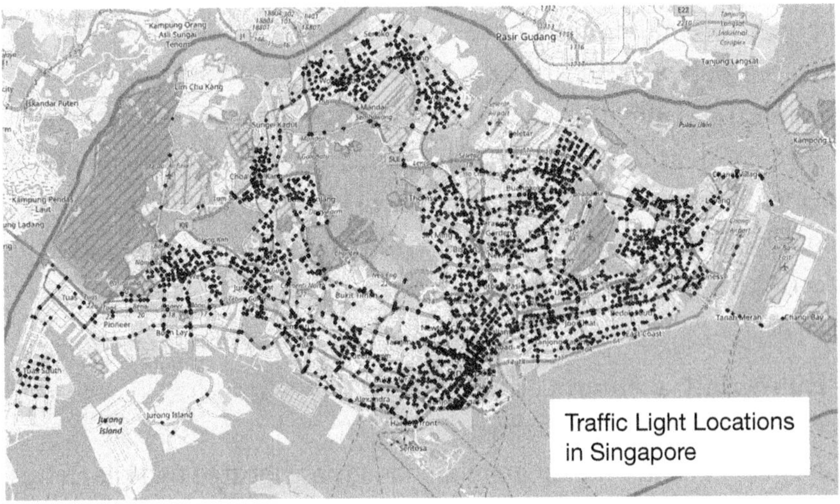

Traffic Light Locations in Singapore

"Once, I drove a passenger to King's Road where Nanyang Primary School is. That's a very good school. Her house faces the school. And she complained how in the morning, she cannot drive her car out to bring her son to the other 'elite' school called Anglo-Chinese School because the road in front of her would be bumper to bumper with cars. It's so hilarious — live so near such a good school yet put her son in another good school, and then complain about the traffic jam because she lives so close to Nanyang Primary.

"And not only that, she complained about having to hear not only the national anthem being played every morning but also the disciplinarian master scolding the children. It was quite funny to hear her complaints. I say then move your son to the school opposite your house. No more headache.

"I would have given anything to exchange our flat for her house. She's sitting on a goldmine to be so near this prestigious school, yet she was complaining about it."

"She's so lucky and doesn't know it," remarked Siew Ling. "You know, some people say living near a school is no good because in Cantonese, 'teach from books' is *gao she* and *she* which means 'books' sounds like 'losing'. So living near a school is no good because it means you lose."

"What nonsense! It's *gao yang* (meaning 'teach to win') for me," came Teng's quick response.

Relocation Effects

"Anyway, what else did Peter say?" asked Siew Ling impatiently.

"He said that when a school announced their upcoming relocation to the public six months before their actual move, prices of private houses located within one kilometre of the original school location went down by almost 3 percent. Those located between one to two kilometres from the old school, went down by 6 percent," Teng responded.

"But if the relocation announcement was made 12 months earlier, the prices went down even sharper with the relocation of the school. Prices of properties within one kilometre of the original school location went down on average by 5.5 percent while those located within the one-to-two-kilometre range declined by almost 7 percent.

"For HDB flats, prices fell too but less so — 0.7 to 1.4 percent."

"You lost me there," cried out a confused Siew Ling. "There are way too many numbers — six months, 12 months, how many percent, and then one kilometre, two kilometres. And then still got private property versus HDB. So confusing. Can write down or not?"

"Ok, ok. This is the summary. Remember, these are properties where the school is originally. And the school is relocating elsewhere," Teng obliged as he wrote down the numbers.

Private Property	Within 1 km	1 to 2 km	
Relocation announced six months before	↓ 3%	↓ 6%	HDB flats ↓ 0.7% to 1.4%
Relocation announced 12 months before	↓ 5.5%	↓ 7%	

"Wow? Went down quite a lot, eh?" said a surprised Siew Ling. "But why did it decline more when the relocation announcement was made 12 months earlier compared to six months earlier?"

"Hmm . . . Peter didn't say. But perhaps there's some gossip already for the six-month announcement? People got wind of the impending move and so were prepared for the news. But for those announced 12 months earlier, maybe the chances of a leak were lower, and so it came as a surprise? I don't know. I'm just guessing," said Teng.

Siew Ling continued with her questions.

"Also, this is for all the schools that were relocated, right? To me, not all schools are good schools. Even our Prime Minister also acknowledged that Singaporeans see different schools differently. I think if a good school were to move, the houses at the original location would see bigger drop in value."

"Wifey, you are sharp," smiled Teng. "The researchers studied exactly the very question you raised. They studied the relocation of schools in the top 50 popularity ranking. And guess what? As you predicted, the prices went down even more when a choice school was to be relocated."

"I knew it," clapped Siew Ling, proud that she was spot on.

"Let me write down the numbers next to these," said Teng as he took back the written paper and scribbled more numbers on it.

Private Property	Within 1 km	1 to 2 km	HDB Flats
Relocation announced six months before	↓ 3%	↓ 6%	HDB flats ↓ 0.7% to 1.4%
Relocation announced 12 months before	↓ 5.5%	↓ 7%	
For good schools that relocated	↓ 8.5%	↓ 12.2%	HDB flats ↓ 5.1% (for less than 1 km); ↓ 2.4% (for 1–2 km)

"If a good school were to be relocated somewhere else, the private houses within one kilometre of its original location saw their value dip by 8.5 percent. Those between one to two kilometres declined by 12.2 percent," explained Teng. "This finding is consistent with the earlier findings, isn't it? Houses between one to two kilometres away from the relocated school are more valued — less traffic jam and less noisy. And so when the school relocates, the housing prices are more affected."

If a good school were to be relocated somewhere else, the private houses within one kilometre of its original location saw their value dip by 8.5 percent. Those between one to two kilometres declined by 12.2 percent.

"But not for HDB flats," observed Siew Ling, as she looked at the numbers on the paper. "Those within one kilometre went down by 5.1 percent compared to 2.4 percent for those one to two kilometres away. Why ah?"

"Hmm . . . Maybe for HDB flats, households are less concerned with noise. They are used to noise already as some inconsiderate neighbours can play TV very loudly or move furniture at night. And maybe they don't drive. They take public transport or walk. So the traffic congestion doesn't really bother them. So being close to a good school is more important to HDB dwellers," Teng hazarded.

"Anyway, these researchers did some more tests and found that this one-to-two kilometre rule of giving primary school registration priority plays a more important factor in driving up prices of private properties than HDB flats."

"Regardless, we hope those good schools near us don't shift out. When they move, we become poorer!" lamented Siew Ling.

"Did Peter say anything about whether an all-girls school, an all-boys school or a co-ed school makes a difference in property prices? I would think a co-ed school is seen to be more 'valuable' because it can accept both boys and girls as students, whereas the same-gender school can only accept either sons or daughters," asked Siew Ling.

"Peter did not say anything about that. But I supposed so," responded Teng. "But you know, I heard from my taxi friends that their kids go to neighbourhood schools and the teachers there are very hardworking. In fact, they say these teachers from neighbourhood schools are even more hardworking than teachers from choice schools because they are aware of their underdog status. So they work harder.

"My taxi friends also say they think teachers from choice schools know the parents are super *kiasu*. Sure to have lots of tuition. So the teachers rely on private tutors to do more coaching. But in neighbourhood schools, there's less money for tuition. So the teachers have to really drill the students on the various subject content. They cannot depend on tutors because not all of their students have tuition."

"I think it would be better for us to do some research on these schools first before we enrol Ethan," said Siew Ling as the couple retired for the day.

WANT TO KNOW MORE?

This chapter is based on Sumit Agarwal, Satyanarain Rengarajan, Sing Tien Foo and Yang Yang, "School Allocation Rules and Housing Prices: A Quasi-Experiment with School Relocation Events in Singapore," *Regional Science and Urban Economics*, Vol. 58, (2016), pp. 42–56. Available at SSRN: https://ssrn.com/abstract=2380761 or http://dx.doi.org/10.2139/ssrn.2380761

Other materials came from www.pmo.gov.sg/content/pmosite/mediacentre/speechsinterviews/primeminister/2013/August/prime-minister-lee-hsien-loong-s-national-day-rally-2013-speech.html

CHAPTER 16

Smoke Gets in Your Eyes

In recent years, Singapore has been affected by the severe smoke haze from forest fires in neighbouring Indonesia.

Forest fires are a frequent occurrence in Southeast Asia especially during dry months. It is also a common practice for farmers to slash and burn as it is a cheap but illegal land-clearing method. In the course of clearing unwanted vegetation and peat, drained peatlands are burnt. With peat being very combustible, these fires do not just occur on the surface of peatlands. They also permeate up to three metres deep underneath the peatlands.

Peatland fires are difficult to put out, especially during the dry El-Nino seasons. The conventional aerial water bombing to put out surface fires is ineffective in dousing peatland fires that occur deep beneath the surface.

The tenacity of such fires also speaks volumes of their uncontrollability. Peatland fires can spread quickly to a large area. Moreover, fires underneath peatlands can resurface and flare up quickly in a short time for an extended period, creating haze that persists for days and weeks.

Haze contains ashes, smoke and dust, as well as toxic pollutants such as $PM_{2.5}$, carbon monoxide and sulfur dioxide, which can cause eye irritation and have damaging long-term effects on the respiratory system if inhaled into the body for a prolonged period. $PM_{2.5}$ measures the level of very fine atmospheric particulate matter.

The Morning After

The alarm went off. Teng woke up with a dry throat and an irritated nose.

"This is strange. Though I did think it was a bit smoky last night, it seems to have gotten worse. Don't tell me got haze again." His sensitive nose began to twitch – a remnant of the asthma attacks he had as a child.

"Last month got haze. And now again," Teng cursed.

He turned on his radio for the latest weather update:

> "Hazy conditions have been persisting in Singapore since last evening, as haze spreading westward from Kalimantan continues to be blown into our region by the prevailing easterly winds. The air quality has been in the 'Very Unhealthy' range since 4 am today. Current conditions are expected to persist for the rest of the day. Singapore has been affected by a prolonged spell of haze this year, with forest fires in Indonesia contributing to the hazy conditions."

"Siew Ling, the haze is back," yelled Teng to his wife who was in the kitchen tending to Ethan. "Remember to stock up on the N95 face masks. Can you buy some at your shopping mall?"

With windows closed and curtains drawn, some of the smoky air had been kept out. Thankfully, they had installed air-conditioning in all their bedrooms when they moved in. That enhanced the comfort of staying at home, especially with Singapore's typical average temperature hovering at 30°C.

"This is like the time when we had the non-stop pounding from the construction of the nearby community centre," thought Teng in a déjà vu moment. Ma and Pa had to keep the windows closed to minimise the construction noise and prevent dust from coming in. "This time, it's the same thing but under different circumstances."

Teng was concerned for Ethan. Just like him when young, his toddler son also suffers from asthma. Last year when there were only a couple of hazy days, Siew Ling and Teng were quite oblivious to Ethan's asthmatic condition. As a result, the boy had turned wheezy with a runny nose.

A year on, they were better prepared. They had bought an air purifier from Courts and planned to keep Ethan at home — no going down to the playground — until the air quality improved.

The air purifier had not come cheap. But they didn't want to take the risk with a young asthmatic child.

It wasn't easy to get one too. Typical Singaporeans, being *kiasu*, had stormed department stores to get them not only for themselves, but also for their father, mother, brother, sister — essentially, everyone in the family. Air purifiers were sold out in most department stores in no time.

Siew Ling was frantic. As a *kiasu* parent, she needed one for Ethan. But thankfully, Teng, with his taxi driver instincts, had figured that areas with less traffic would have less shoppers. He hazarded that the Courts furniture and electronics store at Jurong Point was most likely to have some air purifiers in stock.

He was right. There were just two units left when they got there, and being *kiasu* they bought both. Now, with the haze back, Teng was glad that he made the right decision to get two air purifiers.

"Remember to bring the air purifiers out, just in case," reminded Teng to Siew Ling.

They had planned to bring Ethan to Universal Studios that weekend. He had enjoyed his last visit there. The Sesame Street ride was his favourite. Moreover, meeting the characters from Madagascar had been fun too though he had bawled when his parents wanted to pose with Shrek. Given the haze, it didn't look like this trip was to take place.

Turning to his mother, Teng instructed, "Ma, please don't bring Ethan out. I know it's difficult to be stuck at home but we need to be careful. Not just for Ethan but also for old folks like you and Pa. The government has issued a warning that the very young and elderly should stay at home and minimise any strenuous activity."

Although Ma nodded, Teng knew that she was a stubborn lady and would probably still go out.

On his way out, he bumped into Professor Sing who was leaving for the university.

"Terrible, the haze again," Teng shook his head.

Professor Sing nodded. "But what can we do? We cannot control how the wind blows. And the fires are in Indonesia, outside our jurisdiction."

"You should study what the haze does to us. Not only more people fall sick and spend on medicine, but also use more air-con and go out less. Surely the businesses are affected," grumbled Teng without realising that his suggestion was indeed what Professor Sing was researching on.

Professor Sing smiled.

"If we can't go out, then let's have dinner. How about tomorrow night? We can talk more about the haze," said Professor Sing inviting Teng to his place.

The Haze

In September 2015, Singapore found herself blanketed by smog. Forest fires in Indonesia had generated haze so intense that it shrouded not only their own skies but, because of prevailing winds, Malaysia's and Singapore's as well.

Teng remembered well how the September haze nearly put a stop to Singapore's Grand Prix — the international night race that had put Singapore on the world racing map. As an ardent car enthusiast, he had been looking forward to watching Vettel, Raikkonen and Hamilton, whom he counted as his favourites that weekend.

But the haze had seemed to threaten the drivers' vision and safety, as well as the off-track events and open-air concerts.

Thankfully, a thunderstorm came and the prevailing winds shifted direction, saving Teng's racing-mad weekend. But he could well imagine how much losses the organisers would have incurred if the haze had persisted — not to mention the damage to Singapore's reputation in hosting this international event and as a tourist destination.

But in October, the haze came back with a vengeance. On 19 October 2015, the one-hour $PM_{2.5}$ concentration soared to a record high of 471 $\mu g/m^3$ for western Singapore at 11 pm, while the southern region offered no respite at 301 $\mu g/m^3$ — both way above the normal range of below 55.

Another measure of haze intensity is the Pollutant Standards Index (PSI). PSI above 100 is considered unhealthy, while PSI above 200 is regarded as the very unhealthy range, and PSI above 300 is deemed hazardous. The PSI on that fateful day in October rose from 96 at 9 pm to the very unheathly level of 209 at 11 pm.

The poor visibility of haze-shrouded skies caused the grounding of flights at Changi Airport.

The haze also saw more people visiting medical clinics for a variety of reasons from inflamed eyes, coughs to breathing difficulties. Jobs that required spending long hours outdoors were minimised. People were going out less, which meant that retail shops had literally no sales. In other words, many economic activities came to a grinding halt.

According to the Ministry of the Environment and Water Resources, the 2015 haze was estimated to have caused Singapore $700 million in losses.

Together, these impacted tourism, health and productivity, which in turn translated into economic losses for Singapore. According to the Ministry of the Environment and Water Resources, the 2015 haze was estimated to have caused Singapore $700 million in losses.

Indeed, Teng suffered too. He had far fewer passengers as not many would take to the street with the haze. People just stayed at home.

"Maybe I should just stay at home too. There are so few passengers to pick up," thought Teng. "But if I don't hit the road, there'll be no passengers. No passengers means no money. Yet I have to pay for taxi rental. *Wah piang eh.* And if all taxi drivers think like me, then those poor people who really need a taxi will really suffer. Drive, no good. Don't drive, also no good."

Siew Ling also remarked that her shoe shop was empty. "It was like a ghost town at the mall – same for all the shops; I look at you, you look at me," she laughed about what the shop assistants had been doing since they had no customers, not even window shoppers.

"But at least, I have air-conditioning the whole day. I think that's better than staying at home," Siew Ling shuddered to think of how her in-laws could put up with being cooped up at home with a cranky toddler.

"Oh, but they'll switch on the air-conditioner and the air purifier," Siew Ling remembered. This caused her heart to ache, knowing that her electricity bill would be higher that month.

Dinner with the Sings

Over homemade *yong tou fu*, steamed pomfret, stir-fried *kailan* with mushrooms, crispy pork belly and lotus root soup, the Sing family and their neighbours engaged in an animated discussion about the haze.

The windows were closed and the air-conditioning turned on. The view outside the windows was grey.

"This is so bad. In my 60-plus years, I've never had a haze as bad as this," growled Ma. "It makes us look like a Third World country."

"Tourism will be affected. Our clean and green city is now a dusty and brown city," said Siew Ling. "Today, we had only one customer who came in to the shoe shop, looked around, and after a while, left. She didn't even try the shoes. Luckily I'm not on commission. Otherwise, I think I'll take home just my base pay."

"At the clinic, we had a long waiting line. So many people were down with cough or teary, itchy eyes. We even had a pregnant woman come in, worrying that the haze may affect her unborn child," said Mrs Sing, a nurse at a nearby clinic. "Seems like doctors are one of the few who are doing well during the haze."

"No . . . Mask manufacturers also make money, what!" giggled a mischievous Gillian, Professor Sing's 10-year-old daughter.

"I had to mop the floor so many times even with the windows closed. The dust somehow keeping finding its way in. The pail of water became so dirty so fast. I don't know how many pails of water I've used. And this is only for the floor. I haven't counted cleaning the furniture surfaces yet," barked Ma who was obviously fed up with the haze.

"Urgh . . . Me too," said Mrs Sing, glad that she wasn't the only one complaining about how much water had to be used due to the haze. "And when the haze is over, I'll have to wash the curtains too. And that uses a lot of water as well."

"The good thing about the haze is that we learn not to take clean air for granted. Especially now that we know how bad it can be. So we should learn to conserve and save the Earth," said a wise Pa, calm and collected.

"We can't do much about the haze. We can't force the Indonesian government to ban burning. I heard that because of the wind direction, Jakarta is spared from the haze and thus the politicians are not affected at all," remarked Professor Sing.

"It's so frustrating," returned Teng.

"But we got school holiday!" chirped a cheerful Gillian, oblivious to the economic ramifications of the haze.

"Teng, you remarked yesterday that we should study the effects of the haze on our health, retail sales and the use of air-conditioning," smiled Professor Sing. "You didn't realise it, but my colleagues and I are doing a study now on how the haze affects our use of water and air-conditioning, and therefore, water and energy consumption."

Professor Sing was excited as he talked about his research over dinner. Though somewhat quiet by nature, when it came to discussing research, he could become quite talkative, demonstrating his passion for his work.

"We just started the study. So we haven't completed the analyses yet. We wanted to estimate the economic consequences associated with the haze.

"So we asked PUB (Public Utilities Board) and EMA (Energy Market Authority) for data so that we can study hourly water consumption as well as average monthly electrical consumption for 36 months including the haze period. This will help us assess how we use scarce resources during the haze period and in periods with no haze.

"NEA publishes the air quality in different parts of Singapore, so we can use the appropriate PSI measure for air quality.

"We also wanted to find out how the commercial sector responds whenever a haze occurs. Is there what we call 'economic loss'? So we are also collecting daily hotel performance data which include hotel room rates and occupancy rates.

"And since everyone is on social media these days, we are also collecting social media data from the Twitter accounts of public users during the 36-month period."

"Professor Sing, you said you are working with your colleagues at NUS on this project?" asked Teng.

"Yes. I'm working with my friend Sumit Agarwal," replied Professor Sing.

"The name sounds familiar," wondered Teng. "I think he was one of my passengers many years ago. Is he the one who studied taxi drivers?"

"Ahh . . . yes, that's him. Wow! What a coincidence that he was your passenger and even more amazing, you remembered him!" Professor Sing exclaimed.

"I remember him because he kept asking me how many hours I drive, when I start, when I finish. He asked so many questions but I think what he really wanted to know was how much I earn in a day. But it is a sensitive question to ask.

"Anyway, he shared his findings with me too — that taxi drivers tend to stop work the moment they reach their daily takings or the number of hours they had targeted. That's why sometimes, you cannot find taxis when you need one. They have already met their target for the day. So he was very nice. He advised me that I should think longer term about financial planning.

"And he also advised me that I should not think on a day-to-day basis. If on Monday I didn't hit my income target, then on Tuesday I must work harder. Cannot on Tuesday, just forget about what happened on Monday and still set the same income target. Must make-up for it. Have longer term financial planning. So nice of him to advise me. Can you please say 'Hi' to him for me? Though he probably won't remember me."

"Of course I will," replied Professor Sing.

Three Months Later

Life was back to usual after the weeks of on-and-off haze in September and October. The clear January skies meant people could finally go for their walks and runs.

It was Saturday, and Professor Sing had gone to the wet market with his wife for their weekly grocery shopping. He needed a break after analysing the data he had collected on the haze and utilities consumption. He was drinking his *teh tarik* (Malay for 'pulled tea') at the wet market when he saw Teng also having coffee. "It must be his taxi break time," thought Professor Sing.

"Hey, Teng. Remember the haze study I told you about?" Prof. Sing asked as he approached Teng.

"Ah yes. Is the study completed? What did you find?" asked Teng.

"Come over tonight for dinner and we'll talk. I've much to share with you and my family," said Professor Sing.

The Dinner

Dinner included the *chye sim* freshly bought from Pek Kio wet market, stir fried with garlic. The steamed minced pork was springy with just the right balance of starch, sugar and salt. Mrs Sing was telling Siew Ling how she should slap the marinated minced pork against the plate several times before steaming to get the springy texture. She also reminded her to soak the *tung choy* before mixing it with the minced pork. Mrs Sing was indeed an excellent cook.

"Wah, Mrs Sing. You should be called Singapore's Female Gordon Ramsey," joked Teng. He had been watching the MasterChef series and secretly desired for Siew Ling to cook just as well.

"You are funny. Come, let's eat. Don't be shy," said Mrs Sing as she welcomed the neighbours to a hearty meal.

"Teng, come. I show you this," said Professor Sing as he took out his iPad to show his research findings.

"Urgh . . . This isn't happening," groaned Gillian audibly. What made her dad think that his research was any sort of entertainment to their guests?

"Get a Ph.D. and then you can give your opinion," snapped Mrs Sing in a sharp voice, silencing Gillian with a stern look.

"All of you listen. This is good to know. General knowledge. You should be fortunate that your daddy is a professor who can share his knowledge with you," added Professor Sing as he glared at Gillian.

"Remember when we had the haze and I told you all that I was doing a study on how the haze will impact our water and electricity consumption and the costs to the country? Well, the preliminary results are in."

Professor Sing was grinning from ear to ear, like a little child given a bowl of his favourite candies.

Gillian was far from interested but she didn't want another earful from her parents.

Effect on Water Usage

Like many researchers, Professor Sing was very enthused with his research. "For the water data, we studied almost 400 households living in HDB flats for 36 months including the haze in June 2013.

"As visibility is a key weather characteristic during the haze, we also studied the visibility index. We found that when visibility was halved, or in other words, when the haze level doubled, the average daily water consumption increased by 11 percent.

"We also found that people were more sensitive to the haze when the PSI readings went above 100.

"Look at this chart here. Can you see the big spike in water consumption response? That's the week in June 2013 when we had a week-long haze."

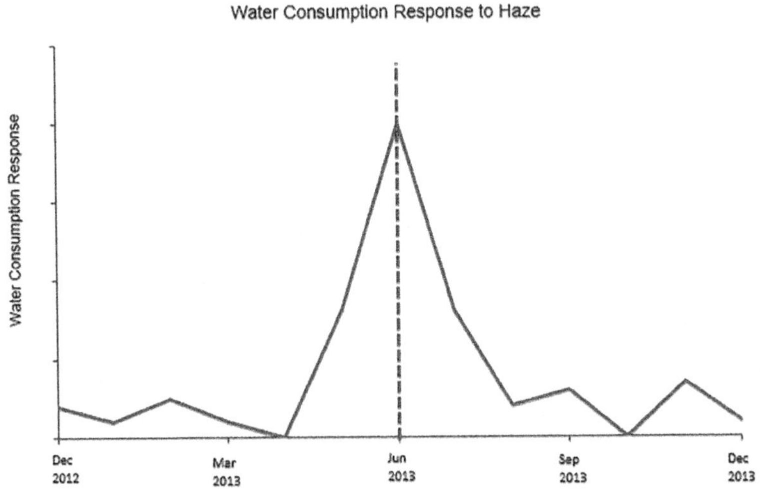

[W]hen visibility was halved, or in other words, when the haze level doubled, the average daily water consumption increased by 11 percent.

"*Wah piang eh*! I thought the haze only made us use more electricity. Water also?" exclaimed Teng. "This haze thing is no joke."

"Wait, I've got more," said Professor Sing as he prepared his guests for more to come.

"Our preliminary findings showed that in terms of water usage, Malay households were more affected by the haze than Chinese and Indian households. Malays used more water during the haze than before the haze, compared to Chinese and Indians.

"Households in bigger flats, such as four-room HDB flats, were also more affected by the haze than three-room HDB flat dwellers."

Everyone listened. They felt somewhat guilty of their higher water consumption during the haze.

"This next set of findings is quite interesting," continued Professor Sing. "We wanted to find out whether the haze would affect the daily activities of Singaporeans, known not only for being *kiasu* but also *kiasee* (meaning 'scared to die').

"So we measured their water consumption for the day from 6 am to 6 pm, and for the night from 6 pm to midnight. We didn't do after midnight till 6 am as most people would be asleep by then, which means water consumption stays low.

"As most people had to commute to school or work and did not stay at home between 6 am to 6 pm on weekdays, the haze did not affect day-time water consumption on weekdays.

"However, at night when people got home from work or school, they used more water for washing off the grime and cleaning dust in the house. So, we found that night-time water consumption increased by about 6 to 9 percent on both weekdays and weekends.

On weekends however, day-time water consumption went up as Singaporeans ... avoided exposure to air pollution by staying at home.

"On weekends however, day-time water consumption went up as Singaporeans, being *kiasee*, avoided exposure to air pollution by staying at home. They minimised health risks by refraining from outdoor activities over the weekends when there's haze."

"What about Twittering? " asked Gillian who is very much into social media.

"Well, we sorted the tweets into three broad categories – Haze, Environment and Health. We also labelled whether the tweets carried a positive or negative emotion.

"We found that when people tweeted more on Environmental issues and exhibited negative emotion such as environmental concern, less water was consumed. Similarly so when Health issues were tweeted. But we didn't find water consumption to be affected by tweets on Haze."

Gillian, who after being admonished by her parents, had been sitting patiently listening to her dad. But she was getting agitated again.

"Mama, can I be excused? I've to do my homework. My school has given us online homework to do and I've to submit it by midnight," asked Gillian, seeking her mum's permission.

"Sure. Just make sure it's homework you're doing. Don't play computer games," warned Mrs Sing.

Effect on Electricity Usage

"Do you want to know the effects of the haze on electricity usage?" asked Professor Sing.

"To see how much the haze induced us to use more electricity, we had the average monthly electricity consumption data for each block for all public and private residential housing blocks including the October 2015 haze period."

Professor Sing swiped his finger across his iPad till he found the correct chart.

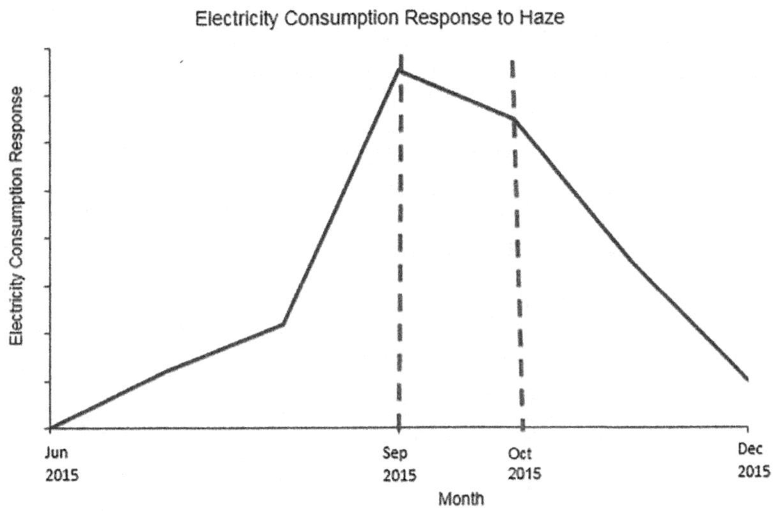

"Take a look at this graph. That's September and October when we had the haze.

"See how the electricity usage spiked during this period? As you expected, more electricity was used during these two months – your air-con, your air purifier, what have you. But the good news is that after the haze was over, usage went down to normal levels. So Singaporeans knew how to adjust."

Everyone nodded.

"How about the hotels? You'd mentioned you also collected data on them," reminded Siew Ling.

"Ah yes," said Professor Sing as he adjusted his glasses. "The data we collected covered about 77 percent of the hotel rooms in Singapore. So it was quite comprehensive and representative of the hotel industry here. Well, not only did hotel occupancy rate go down, but room rates also went down during the haze."

The Bottomline

"It's all fascinating but I'm a little lost with so many numbers," acknowledged Teng that he had difficulty following all the findings.

"Yes, yes . . . It can get quite difficult to understand. There's a lot of information to digest, isn't it?" said Professor Sing.

"Let me try to put it in a nutshell.

"If we have a terrible haze, say PSI jumps from 50 to 300, the daily water consumption per household will go up by about 25 percent, while the monthly electricity consumption per block will go up by a whopping 40 percent.

If ... PSI jumps from 50 to 300, the daily water consumption per household will go up by about 25 percent, while the monthly electricity consumption per block will go up by a whopping 40 percent.

"Using a back-of-the-envelope method of calculation . . . "

"Eh . . . Professor Sing, sorry, but what is 'back-of-the-envelope'?" enquired Teng.

"Ah . . . 'back-of-the-envelope' calculation means a rough calculation," explained Professor Sing.

"As I was saying, we did a back-of-the-envelope calculation. We calculated how much additional water would be used and multiplied it by the appropriate tariff rates. We did the same for electricity.

"If the PSI went up by 100 percent, the cost of the haze would be $2.6 million for additional water used and $8 million for increases in electricity usage.

If the PSI went up by 100 percent, the cost of the haze would be $2.6 million for additional water used and $8 million for increases in electricity usage.

"If the PSI went up by 500 percent, the cost of the haze would be $13 million for extra water consumed and $40 million for additional electricity used.

"So if the haze comes and the PSI doubles, we would expect households to be spending easily $10.6 million more on water and electricity."

"What? This is ridiculous," cried Teng. "We *kena* spending so much more when we didn't create the haze? It isn't our fault. And we haven't even taken into account the losses by companies. I won't be surprised if the haze costs us hundreds of millions in losses. And we also haven't considered long-term health impacts."

"Yes, that's a lot of money," responded Professor Sing. "I'm not making light of the situation but for comparison, the haze caused Indonesia an economic loss of about $20 billion!"

"Put an end to haze!" shouted Teng, thumping his fist in the air.

Teng's Question

"Professor, I've a question . . .," stumbled Teng as he tried his best to string his words together, hoping that the question didn't sound too silly. He had been wanting to seek the professor's advice on this work-related issue for a long time.

"All this haze is pollution from forest fires. How about pollution from car engine? Like I drive my blue taxi. I make good money. But my *kiasu* friends keep telling me to go to Changi Airport to pick up passengers.

They say there are many passengers there — tourists, Singaporeans, anyone who lands at Changi Airport. But I must queue for a long time. There's a long line of taxis waiting at the airport. And my taxi friends leave the air-con on while waiting. Do you think it is worth queuing in line for the airport passenger or not?"

Professor Sing considered Teng's question and responded.

"Well, there are two aspects to your question. From your perspective, as a driver, you want to know whether waiting long in the airport queue with the air-con on is worth the fare the passenger pays.

"From the policy perspective, the question is whether waiting in the long line with the air-con switched on contributes to air pollution and the faster deterioration of the car, and ultimately do more harm than good to the environment.

"Let's tackle your perspective first.

"You'll need to consider opportunity cost."

"What is that, ah?" asked Teng.

"In your case, your opportunity cost is how much money could you have made by picking up passengers not at Changi Airport but elsewhere in Singapore. But because you are waiting in line at the airport, you would have given up these other potential passengers for the airport passengers.

"So, say you waited in line for one hour and later spend half an hour driving the airport passenger to his destination. That's 1.5 hours. In that 1.5 hours, you could have gotten maybe three other passengers on the road elsewhere. Maybe their fares could have come up to $35. I think that's a reasonable estimate, right? It would be higher if it's peak period. Now, for it to be worth your while to wait so long at the airport, your airport passenger must incur a cab fare of more than

$35. If you are *sway*, and that guy lives near the airport, then you *habis lah* (meaning 'unfortunate finishing') – you get maybe only $10. And on top of that, you have to lug the heavy luggage into your boot. No joke, right?"

Everybody laughed.

Teng thought, "With my stupid luck, I won't be surprised if this happens," as memories of the cohort size effect still haunted him.

Professor Sing continued, "You must also consider that with the engine switched on for an hour, you'll incur more petrol costs and wear-and-tear to the taxi. All these add up.

"Now, let's look from the bigger perspective. How would having so many taxis queuing at the airport help people and the society? You may be right in that there might be more fumes from idle engine running.

"But there would also be fewer taxis on the road to pick up non-airport passengers with many of you waiting at the airport. So these non-airport passengers cannot find a taxi easily.

"So from an environmental point of view, it's not good to have so many taxis idling. Not just because of pollution but also it's a wasteful use of petrol.

"From a societal point of view, it's not good to have people in the rest of Singapore waiting and waiting for taxis when they need one.

"Now, considering the viewpoint of taxi company and driver, is the fare from the airport passenger worth all these costs?"

Teng replied, "Prof., maybe this can be your next research project."

"It might well be, Teng. It might well be," smiled Professor Sing.

WANT TO KNOW MORE?

This chapter is based on Sumit Agarwal, Sing Tien Foo and Yang Yang, "Risk Avoidance and Environmental Hazard: Effects of the Transboundary Haze Pollution in Singapore," (15 March 2017). Available at SSRN: https://ssrn.com/abstract=2942096 or http://dx.doi.org/10.2139/ssrn.2942096

Other materials came from "Haze Episode Cost Singapore Estimated S$700 million: Masagos," *Channel News Asia*, (15 March 2016). http://www.channelnewsasia.com/news/singapore/haze-episode-cost-singapore-estimated-s-700m-last-year-masagos-8147924

CHAPTER 17

Girl, Shower Faster, Save Water

Sarah felt quite good having educated her mum on the energy conservation study that she had learnt about in school a year ago — that mere nudging from family members can motivate people to take steps towards saving electricity. Her mum, mindful of the environment, appreciated learning from her about the NEA study.

She was particularly smug because she had been on the receiving end of advice from her mother. Her mum had been bugging her on her tendency to take long showers.

"Sarah, why are you still in the bathroom? Quickly finish your shower. Don't waste water," reminded her mum on an almost daily basis.

Especially during the haze periods, Sarah had been using more water than usual to get the polluted dirt out from every part of her body. She recalled how bad it was during the last haze. She could feel the dust on each and every fine hair on her body, though her mum had written it off as a product of her vivid imagination. "Urgh," she cringed at the irksome thought. She was only too glad that her school had been closed for the day.

"Oh! I love the cool water splashing on me," Sarah's face lighted up as she thought of getting herself cleaned and smelling good after an entire day in school. It helped to refresh herself and that was what she wanted before she had her dinner and started on her school homework.

"No five-minute showers for me," insisted Sarah. She thought that showering fast would not make a person clean.

To her, showering was a ritual where each step had to be slowly carried out and thoroughly enjoyed. She loved the exotic scent of her shower gel, a combination of Hawaiian flowers and herbs – pikake with awapuhi and kukui oil – as she slowly swathed her tanned skin until it was covered with the rich luxurious foam.

Sarah remembered how, when she had first showered all by herself at three years old, she would make bubbles with her shower gel. The iridescent rainbow of colours reflected from the bubbles amid the rain shower falling gently on her back captivated her. She would try to make as huge a bubble as possible. Her showers were her play time – and long ones at that.

Now a teenager, she still enjoyed pampering herself with bubble making occasionally.

Part of her showering ritual involved a very careful and systematic washing between her toes and behind her ears using the shower scrub Mum had bought for her last Christmas. Every toe nail was also to be carefully brushed to get rid of dirt that gathered during the hours they spent inside her school shoes.

Her long hair needed that special pampering too. Using sulfate-free shampoo, Sarah was careful that she gave her hair a gentle but dedicated wash to remove all the grime without too much hair falling off. After a thorough rinsing to make sure there was no shampoo residue left, she finished off with a hair treatment from Japan designed to get rid of tangles and protect her hair from the harsh effects of colouring and the sun. All that required another round of complete rinsing.

And all this while, Sarah would be belting out the latest Ed Sheeran or Katy Perry songs. Her voice always sounded better in the bathroom than the bedroom.

"Why doesn't Mum understand that this is just about the only time I can truly relax from the stress of school and have some brief respite from Singapore's humid weather? My sanity is more important than saving water," Sarah always wondered.

In contrast, Josie wondered why Sarah didn't seem to understand and change her wasteful showering behaviour. Sometimes, she asked herself where had she gone wrong as a mother in not inculcating a sense of responsibility in her daughter.

"Teenagers," Josie thought as she rolled her eyes.

Water and Singapore

Water is an important and scarce resource in Singapore. Long-term self-sustainability has been one of the key strategic thrusts in Singapore's blueprint of water supply.

It has developed a sustainable water supply system tapping from four sources known as The Four National Taps — local catchment areas, imported water from Malaysia, reclaimed water and desalinated water — to meet the long-term needs of water for the five-million strong populace.

However, securing an adequate water supply alone is not enough. Singapore also needs to manage water demand and conservation.

Over the years, efforts at water conservation have seen Singapore's water consumption per capita fall. The target is to reduce per capita water consumption to 140 litres a day by 2030.

In Singapore, showering uses about 30 percent of an average family's monthly water consumption. If households can change their behaviour during showers, substantial savings in water consumption can be achieved.

In Singapore, showering uses about 30 percent of an average family's monthly water consumption. If households can change their behaviour during showers, substantial savings in water consumption can be achieved.

The Blow-up

Josie came back from work, not at all happy as there had been another train breakdown again. She had brought work home to do, thinking that she could have dinner at home and subsequently attend to her work while keeping an eye on Sarah, to make sure the latter did her homework.

The breakdown had wreaked havoc on transportation logistics. What would usually be a 45-minute ride home took Josie almost two hours. With a splitting headache, she came back and found Sarah napping.

"Hey, sweetie. Wake up. Quickly take your shower and we'll go out for dinner," said Josie as she gave Sarah a gentle pat. A sleepy-eyed Sarah rose and headed for the shower.

Fifteen minutes passed. "Where's Sarah?" thought Josie. She was still taking her shower.

"Hey, hurry up. I'm hungry. Why take so long to shower?" Josie raised her voice outside the bathroom so that Sarah could hear her amid the pitter-patter of the shower.

Another 15 minutes passed. Sarah was still showering.

"Sarah, don't waste water. Quickly finish your shower. We need to go for dinner!" shouted a fuming Josie, this time competing against her daughter's singing on top of the sound of running water.

"Thank goodness I don't have a bath tub. I can't imagine how much my water bill will be then," grumbled Josie.

Five minutes later, Sarah emerged with an unrepentant look and pursed lips.

Josie continued to barrage her daughter on the need to be considerate – to not keep people waiting, and to also save the environment by not wasting water.

"Remember what our neighbour Professor Sing said about Singaporeans using too much water?" Josie interrogated her daughter.

But all Sarah heard was "blah blah blah". Josie had been harping on saving water all these years that Sarah had grown immune to her mum's incessant nagging, even though it came with good intentions.

"What's she going to do? Cut off the water supply?" thought the sassy millennial.

Pre-study

One day, Josie received a letter from PUB that her household had been selected to be part of a national study on understanding ways to encourage people to conserve water.

"I wonder whether this is part of Professor Sing's research. Regardless, this is exactly what Sarah needs – a wake-up call," thought Josie as she was at wits' end as to what else to do to get her daughter not to waste water when showering. Without any hesitation, she signed up for it.

The campaign involved fixing a smart shower device to the shower head. The device would provide feedback during each shower based on real-time information. With a programmable volume display, the device would show the volume of water used. Based on water usage goals set by the user, the tracking of targets would be notified through an animation with accompanying messages – either 'Very Good', 'OK', or 'Too Much'. Additionally, the device could also record flow rate, duration of shower and temperature.

Josie was committed to taking part in this study. She wanted the smart shower device to be installed in Sarah's bathroom. But she wasn't sure how Sarah would react.

A few weeks later, the research team from PUB visited Josie's home to install the device. They told Josie that she could set one of five goals for water consumption during showering – 10, 15, 20, 25 or 35 litres.

Mindful that she wanted Sarah to use less water without setting an unachievable target, Josie chose '20 litres'.

Josie had told the neighbours that she was taking part in the PUB study. Siew Ling said she wasn't notified about it. Mrs Sing said they couldn't take part because her husband was among the group of professors involved in the study.

"I'm so glad that I was chosen. This is so timely," Josie thought.

The Study Begins

When Sarah came from school, she was surprised to see the device in her bathroom. Josie was hoping that she wouldn't be put off and start sulking again. Sarah didn't. In fact, she was quite taken by the device.

"Cool," Sarah said when Josie explained the purpose of the device to her and what it can do. "Wow! So smart!"

"And the water target set is 20 litres. The PUB man says 20 litres is a reasonable target. Some households have 15 or even 10 litres," explained Josie. "And if you shower using 20 litres or less, there'll be a picture of a happy polar bear. Earth is saved.

"But if you use more than 20 litres, that's no good for Earth. The ice will melt and there'll be no polar bears left. You will also get the message 'Too Much'."

"No problem, Mum. I can achieve the target. Easy peasy," answered a confident Sarah.

She was excited to try the device. Furthermore, she couldn't wait to tell her friends that she had been specially selected to participate in this study to help the nation conserve water.

Her first shower was quite interesting. Her eyes kept fixated on the device to see how much water she was using. Showering became more mindful.

"What?" Sarah was stunned at how fast the numbers were running as water flowed from the showerhead. "I'm already at 15 litres? I haven't even rinsed off the shampoo."

She couldn't believe she had used so much water already.

She tried to 'fast forward' her showering to meet the 20-litre target that she had assuredly told her mum she could achieve. But by the time she finished her shower, she had used 35 litres of water – a staggering 15 litres more than the target.

"Hmm . . . Either something's wrong with this device or my mum would also be using almost the same amount of water as I do," thought Sarah, trying to protect her ego and think of how to defend against her mother's claim of excessive water usage.

"Well, how did you do?" Josie was standing outside the bathroom, eagerly awaiting to find out how Sarah fared.

"Mum, I think the device is faulty. Can you shower in my bathroom? I want to see how much water you use. And shower like you usually do. Don't try to purposely use less water. I won't tell you how much I consumed yet. We can compare our performance after you've showered," said a somewhat defiant Sarah.

Josie obliged to prove the point that Sarah was using way too much water. When she came out of the bathroom, she jokingly said with a 'sad' facial expression, "22 litres. And the polar bears died."

"Oh Mum! 22 litres? Well, that's two litres more than the target. So you need to use less water," shook Sarah's head.

"And how about you?" challenged Josie.

"Mum, you're right. I used way too much water. I couldn't believe my eyes. It was a whopping 35 litres. 35 litres! I used so much?" declared Sarah with disbelief written all over her face.

"But Mum, what is 35 litres? I know 35 litres is too much. But what does 35 litres mean?"

Josie, with a flash of brilliance, said, "Well, you know we are encouraged to drink at least two litres of water each day. You know what two litres is, don't you? The jug of water we have?" referring to the jug they kept in the kitchen to help Sarah visualise what two litres entailed.

"So using 35 litres of water means you're using 17.5 days of water that could have been used for drinking.

"Put it another way – we've set the target as 20 litres for showering. Assuming you achieve that target, it means each shower you take is tantamount to 10 days of drinking.

"Now if it were an 'either/or' situation where you either have drinking water or showering water, which would you choose – one shower in 20 days with no water to drink during that period or 20 days of drinking water but no shower?

"I think that will help emphasise the importance of not wasting water, especially when showering."

That analogy stuck with Sarah. She didn't think she could live 20 days without drinking water. She would die. But she wouldn't die for not showering for 20 days.

Months Ahead

In the next few months, Sarah was very conscientious of how she showered. She would turn off the faucet when she was lathering. She was amazed at how much water she could save through just the simple act of turning the shower head off.

She also realised that she didn't need to turn the faucet to the full volume to rinse off. When turned to the maximum flow, some of the water wasn't on her anyway. What a waste!

Sarah also used less shower gel, shampoo and hair treatment. She realised that the more she used, the longer it took to rinse off. That again helped to save more water.

She also learnt that sometimes, all it needed was just a little more water to get the foamy lather that she loved. "Wow! I'm saving water and shower gel too," Sarah thought.

Slowly but surely, Sarah achieved the 20-litre goal that her mum had set.

But feeling unsatisfied with that, she had told herself that she's going to prove to her mother that she can do one better — she'll try to shower with less than 18 litres, nearly half the 35 litres that she used when she first started using the smart shower device.

One day, the PUB research team visited to check that the smart water device was still working fine and to obtain any feedback that Josie or Sarah might have.

With Josie and Sarah's somewhat bubbly personalities, they engaged with the researchers on how they tried to save water. In response, the researchers were more than willing to share with them some preliminary findings that might encourage them to save even more.

The Findings

"Over 500 households were fitted with this smart shower device and their recordings were taken over four to six months. They were divided into seven groups," said one of the researchers.

"Group 1, which is what we call the Control Group, had the device fitted but only saw the water temperature. They did not receive any feedback on how much water they used and no water usage goal was set.

"Group 2 consisted of households who were given feedback on how much water they were using. But they were not given any targets in saving water.

"Groups 3 to 7 were households who, in addition to receiving feedback, were also given water usage targets to achieve. Groups 3 and 4 were given challenging targets of 10 and 15 litres, Group 5 had a realistic target of 20 litres, while Groups 6 and 7 had easy targets of 25 and 35 litres, respectively."

"Ahh . . . So we are in Group 5," said Sarah.

"That's right. And your mum told us that with the device, you've actually learned to shower faster and use water more efficiently. That's excellent to know," said the researcher.

"This graph will help you see how much water was used for showering over the course of the six-month study," said the researcher as he whipped out a laminated graph with colourful jagged lines.

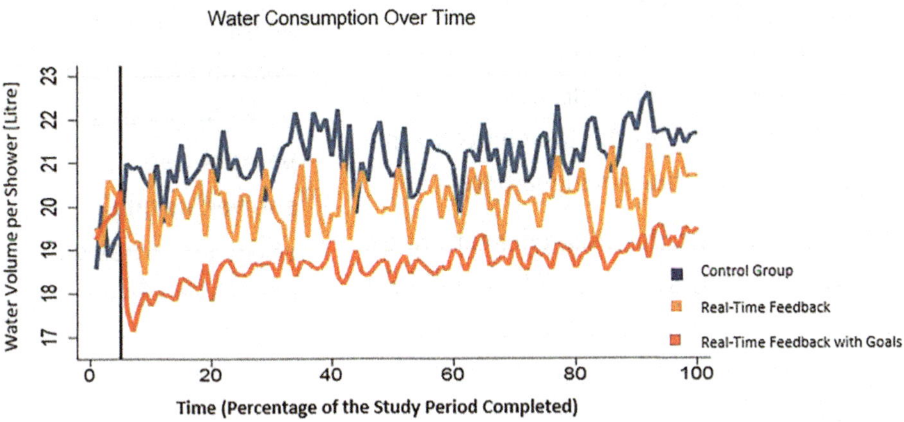

"Look at Time '0' at the bottom left. That is the start of the study. You can see that all households start at about the same volume of water used for showering. For the first 20 showers prior to providing feedback, Singaporeans use almost 20 litres of water in a single shower that takes up about five minutes. This is the average amount of water used per shower.

"But as the study progresses, you see a divergence. Your household is reflected in the red line – households that received real-time feedback and with a goal to achieve. These are the best. You see that they used much less water than the Control Group (blue line) – the group that received no feedback and had no water conservation goal. The next best water conservers are those who only received feedback on how much water they were using when showering with no water conservation goal (orange line).

"When there was feedback given regarding their water usage, we found that water consumption went down by about 10 percent per shower, saving about two litres of water per shower. That's enough for drinking in a day.

"So we learnt that giving feedback and setting targets motivate people to conserve."

When there was feedback given regarding ... water usage, ... water consumption went down by about 10 percent per shower, saving about two litres of water per shower.

Sarah pondered, "This reminds me very much of how my teachers will give me feedback when I don't do well in my tests and set targets for me to achieve for my next test. It's the same idea here."

"Not only that," the researcher continued. "You'll see that the saving behaviour continues over time. Remember that this study was conducted over four to six months. That's quite a long while.

"Some people may say that the new behaviour of using less water is only temporary and cannot be sustained over time. We haven't finished collecting all the data but our preliminary findings show this isn't the case. After four months or about the 80 and 100 percent time mark of the study, the water-conserving behaviour of Groups 3 to 7 can still be observed."

"Do you mean everyone in Groups 3 to 7 saved water? How can setting at 35 litres as an objective be called saving water?" enquired Sarah who felt she had to work pretty hard to meet her 20-litre target compared to someone in the 35-litre target group.

"I'm about to come to that. Thanks for bringing it up. Let's see," the researcher flipped to another laminated graph.

"This is the graph that addresses your question. It shows the change in water volume used, in other words, how much water was saved for different groups.

"The Control Group fared the worst. Not only did they not save, they actually used more. The group that saved the most water is the group

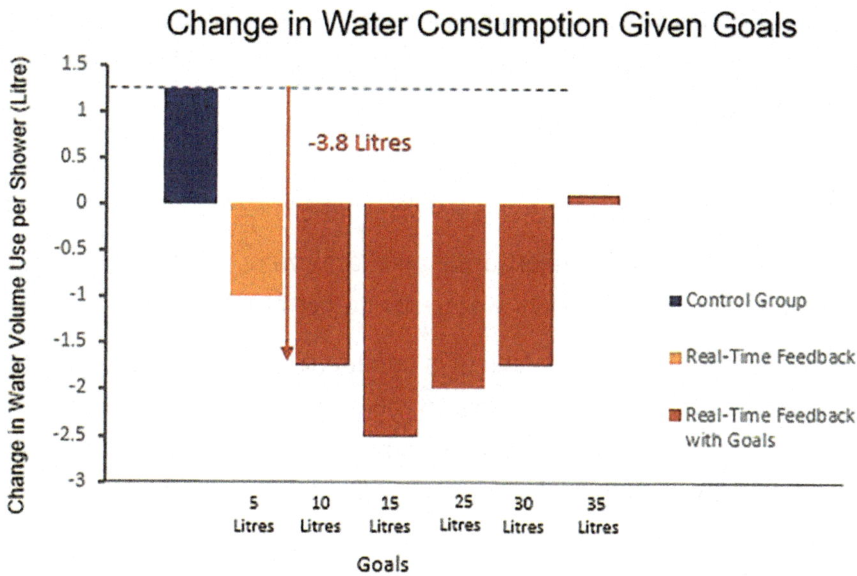

who set 15 litres as their target. They saved about 3.8 litres per shower, giving a saving of about 19 percent. The ambitious target of 10 litres was also effective though to a lesser degree with 2.9 litres of water saved during a shower. I think because these were relatively challenging targets to achieve, these households pushed themselves to achieve the target. So they worked harder to save water.

The group that saved the most water is the group who set 15 litres as their target. They saved about 3.8 litres per shower, giving a saving of about 19 percent.

"Your group, 20 litres, is the second best performer. Good job! But you can do better as 20 litres is just about the average water consumption per shower.

"You asked about households in the group with a 35-litre target. Like you said, setting 35 litres as the target is like not saving water at all. Indeed, these households did not change how much water they used for showering."

"Wow! This is stunning," said an amazed Josie. She was so glad that her household had been chosen to take part and that Sarah had been willing to co-operate too.

Reflections

After the research team left, Josie and Sarah were still chatting about the findings and their own water-saving performance.

"This is like how annual review is conducted in my office. I have to sit down with those reporting to me and together, we set annual targets for them to achieve. I also have semi-annual reviews to give them feedback and motivate them to do better," said Josie.

"Yes, it does look like goal setting and feedback are keys to performance even in the often-thought ill-disciplined area of water conservation," responded Sarah. She was beginning to feel a different sense of responsibility and achievement — that she could do something about water conservation and yet enjoy her showers.

"So Mum, targets set must be within reach to motivate people to strive hard to attain them. When a target is either too ambitious (e.g., below 10 litres), it may be discouraging. If it is too easily attainable (e.g., above 30 litres), it becomes ineffective in encouraging households to save water.

[T]argets set must be within reach to motivate people to strive hard to attain them. When a target is either too ambitious (e.g., below 10 litres), it may be discouraging. If it is too easily attainable (e.g., above 30 litres), it becomes ineffective in encouraging households to save water.

"I really think that PUB should install such devices in all

households and set appropriate targets and feedback. I think Singaporeans can be persuaded to be more conscious about saving water. I, for one, am testimony that it can be done. Our behaviour can be modified and hopefully, this would become a sustainable lifestyle change.

"And we should have two types of taps – one for potable water which is for drinking, and another for non-potable for washing clothes and cleaning. So the non-potable can be from rain that doesn't need to go through too much of a purification process. Saves cost.

"We should also think about energy conservation. Why aren't we investing more into solar energy? We get the sun 12 hours a day, 365 days a year. It's perfect. When I went on a school trip to Tokyo, I saw some buildings with solar panels for energy. And I thought to myself why isn't Singapore capitalising on its geographical location and weather – turn the sunny weather which is a bane in some instances into an advantage?

"And perhaps this smart water device can be extended beyond water conservation. How about electricity conservation? We can install a smart electricity device that monitors how much turning the air-conditioning on costs us. Remember the haze period? The air-con was switched on almost the whole day. Sorry, Mum that I used so much energy."

"My, my," thought Josie with a smile. "My daughter is growing up after all."

"Hey! How about going to Hoshino Coffee for dinner? We can have your favourite *matcha* souffle for dessert," offered Josie.

"And blended fruit tea?" asked Sarah.

"Certainly," came the reply as Josie gave her daughter a big hug.

WANT TO KNOW MORE?

This chapter is based on Sumit Agarwal, Lorenz Goette, Sing Tien Foo, Verena Tiefenbeck and Davin Wang Hong Yip, "Real Time Information in Water Consumption Behaviour of Households in Showers," (2016). Working Paper, National University of Singapore; and Sumit Agarwal and Sing Tien Foo, "Targets, Real-time Feedback Can Cut Water Use in the Shower," *The Straits Times*, (11 February 2017). http://www.straitstimes.com/opinion/targets-real-time-feedback-can-cut-water-use-in-the-shower

CHAPTER 18

Auntie, We Paint Your Flat

"Yesterday, two men from the Town Council came and changed the lights outside our flat," Ma told Teng one Saturday morning before he began his taxi shift.

"They changed everyone's lights along the corridor. Pa asked them why. They said this type of lights saves more energy."

"That's good. Maybe we should change ours also. I don't know whether ours is LED or not," Teng said.

"Aiyoh! LED lights are expensive. I also heard they spoil faster. Don't know true or not. First, pay more for the lights, then save when using. But we don't know how long the lights can *tahan*. If they don't last long, then perhaps in the end we spend even more," said a hesitant Siew Ling.

"Besides, we already have the water-saving washing machine, right? We've already done our part to save the environment."

A few weeks later, each household received a letter from the Town Council which was established to manage and maintain the common areas in the estate. The letter informed the respective households that the estate was due for a new coat of exterior paint. In Singapore, HDB blocks are painted about every five years to protect the exterior from the harsh elements of sun and rain.

Teng's block would be the first to be painted in a month's time. Information on the painting schedule and instructions on drying their washed clothes indoors and keeping their windows closed were given. The letter also notified Teng and his neighbours that a special type of paint would be used — one that is reflective and purportedly can insulate the building from heat, thus saving on energy consumption.

"That means we don't have to draw the curtains all the time. With windows and curtains closed, the rooms can become so stuffy," said Ma.

"And remember we thought of putting solar film on our bedroom windows to cut down the glare and heat? Maybe we should wait first and see whether our house is cooler with the new paint. If it becomes cooler, then we don't have to put the screen," said Teng.

Painting Starts

The day of painting came. As per usual practice, most of the HDB dwellers left their shoes outside their flat — though there was a concern that the painting work would cause stains on the shoes. In addition, some residents were worried that shoes might go missing with strangers walking around. Ma was urging her neighbours to bring their footwear into their flat.

"Better lah. You never know, these shoes could get stained by the paint. Then what do you do? Buy more shoes? That would be wasting money," advised Ma to Josie and Mrs Sing. Ma had always been the *kiasu* one with an aversion to wasting money.

The neighbours also moved their potted plants away from the corridor walls to make it easier for the painters to do their job.

"Hi Mrs Sing. Wow! Your plants look so healthy. You're good at gardening eh," complimented Teng as he looked at the potted pandan, chilli, and aloe vera. He then remembered Mrs Sing to be a great cook and asked, "You grow them for your cooking?"

"Thank you, Teng," responded Mrs Sing. "Yes, I try to grow some organic herbs that I can use for cooking."

"This painting . . . It's supposed to make the flat less hot. I hope so. Then we don't have to use so much air-con," chatted Teng.

"That would be good. Climate change is very real. There's global warming. We can do with using less electricity and water," joined Josie in the conversation.

"Did you know, the other day, some men came to change the corridor lights?" asked Teng. "They said that the new type of lights will save electricity."

"I've changed the lights in my house to LED lights already," offered Josie.

"Josie, do you remember that time when you took part in the PUB study on saving water? I think the government was collecting information on the amount of water used. We cannot be forever relying on Malaysia to supply us with water. Yet, Singaporeans take water supply for granted," said Mrs Sing. "I think sooner or later, water price will go up. It's only a matter of time."

"Maybe. And perhaps electricity prices will be jacked up too. That's why the government is changing to these energy-saving lights and insulation paint to reduce electricity usage," added Josie. "I wonder whether all these efforts will really save energy. *Sekali* (used for emphasis to demonstrate the contradictory behaviour that may occur) people use even more electricity because they mistakenly think they are already using less with these energy-saving devices."

"Let me ask my husband. He always has this study and that study," volunteered Mrs Sing. "The other day, I heard him mention that Singapore's masterplan is to have at least 80 percent of buildings be green by 2030. So I think he may know something about it."

Green Mark Rating

Concerns over global warming have led to active environmental movements promoting energy-efficient buildings. In 2005, Singapore became the first Asian country to adopt the Green Mark rating system to evaluate the environmental impact and performance of buildings. Managed by the Building and Construction Authority (BCA), it measures how well a building reduces water and energy consumption and improves indoor environmental quality. A building can be certified with one of four rating levels: BCA Green Mark Platinum, Gold^{Plus}, Gold and Certified.

Singapore plans to have at least 80 percent of its buildings green by 2030 and be a global leader in green buildings with special expertise in the tropics and sub-tropics.

As Singapore plans to have at least 80 percent of its buildings green by 2030 and be a global leader in green buildings with special expertise in the tropics and sub-tropics, there are several funding and incentive schemes to motivate developers to adopt green building technologies and environmentally friendly construction practices, especially in the private sector. Thus far, the response has been good.

Are Green Buildings Really 'Green'?

"Sing, HDB painting started today. So please be careful when you go to work tomorrow. Don't blind blind knock onto the gondola," said Mrs Sing as she started the conversation over dinner.

"Hmm . . .," was her husband's response, engrossed in reading a research working paper while eating.

"Eh, Sing ah. I'm talking to you," said Mrs Sing. "Are you listening or not?"

"Listening. I can eat, read and listen at the same time," said Professor Sing as he continued reading, without lifting his head to talk to his wife.

"HDB said it is using a special paint that helps to insulate the flat from the heat. Apparently, it can cut the temperature down by one or two degrees," said an exasperated Mrs Sing trying to get her husband's attention.

"Hmm . . .," came the reply.

"The other day, HDB came to change the corridor lights to the energy-saving type," she continued. Still, her husband remained uninterested in the conversation.

"Our neighbour, Josie, asked whether making a building green actually means the consumption of less energy.

"I remembered you mentioned before about green buildings. Has anyone done research on them?"

Suddenly, Professor Sing looked up and showed some interest. His wife had mentioned the magic word — research.

"I don't know of any research on this. There could be but I don't know," her husband replied.

"Why don't you research on this?" Mrs Sing encouraged her husband.

"Maybe, we'll see," was the reply. "If I were to do that, what would you be interested to find out?"

"I think something like whether the cost of constructing green buildings is justified by the savings in energy and water bills. Like how many years of savings does it take before the cost of greening is recovered."

"Hmm . . . So you're talking about cost-benefit analysis and breakeven. That's good. What else?" asked Professor Sing as he started soliciting ideas from his wife to assess whether the study would be potentially interesting to Singaporeans and policy makers.

"I would also be interested to know whether there are different types of 'green'. I don't think all green buildings are the same. Some may be more green than others. So what are these various types of green building? And are they very different in terms of their impact on environmental friendliness.

"Also, I want to know which is more important — saving on electricity or saving on water. I think there may be a situation of give-and-take. Greening cannot be for everything, right? Otherwise it would be extremely expensive.

"Then I also want to know which type of greening measures saves more electricity, and what type saves more water. If I were a house buyer, I would want to know this, so that I know which type to buy. If I'm the type who spends a lot on electricity using the computer and watching TV and doesn't spend a lot on water, then I would prefer a particular type of green house. If I spend more on water — gardening my plants, maintaining an aquarium, taking long showers — but less on electricity, then I'll be more interested in another type of green house," explained his wife.

The next day, Mrs Sing updated Josie.

"I asked my husband. He says he's not aware of any study done on green buildings. But I urged him to start one," Mrs Sing laughed.

"Maybe he will because he started asking me what I would be interested to know," Mrs Sing continued. "You've got any ideas?"

Josie thought for a while.

"Hmm . . . I guess you would have told him the usual already – how much does greening actually save the household.

"Let me think . . . How about the haze? We had the haze last time. And who knows we may have more periods like that in the future. Remember how we had to close our windows and turn on the air-conditioning? So I'd be interested to know how much an environmentally friendly house would save on their energy bill when the house has to go on heavy duty energy during the haze.

"I guess my question is about people who use very little energy – say husband and wife with no kids, both working long hours in the office and are hardly at home. Is it worth it for them to buy a green house? I can see that it is possible for large families who use a lot of electricity and water to benefit from an energy-saving house. But for smaller families? So when would it make investing in a green home worth the while? How much electricity must you consume before the savings start to kick in?"

"Good questions. I'll tell Sing these tonight," thanked Mrs Sing.

Josie smiled to herself as she thought, "There'll soon be another dinner and the topic will be on energy saving."

WANT TO KNOW MORE?

This chapter is based on Sumit Agarwal, Sing Tien Foo and Yang Yang, "Are Green Buildings Really 'Green'? – Energy Efficiency of Green Mark Labels in Singapore," (2017). Working Paper, National University of Singapore.

CHAPTER 19

Vegetable Seller, Why So Expensive?

"Nowadays, Singapore is so expensive. Taxi fares go up, water bills go up, now food prices also go up," said a disgruntled Ma as she unpacked her groceries to put the fresh pieces of meat and vegetables into the refrigerator.

"This piece of pork costs $30. *Mai yao yu* (a high-end fish) costs $65 a kilo! And the *kailan* – $3 for this small bunch of vegetables. And I had to buy two bunches because one is not enough for four adults. So expensive. Now every bite must be a golden bite."

Teng had been giving his parents $500 every month to help pay for groceries and household items. He could not give more. There were still the utilities, Ethan's daycare fees, and the massive housing loan to pay; not forgetting his own self-imposed savings – 'Teng's Pension Fund', as he called it.

As a taxi driver, he was not entitled to CPF, and so could not rely on that when he hit retirement. He also had to stash aside some cash for rainy days. He still remembered Professor Agarwal's advice on financial planning for his taxi takings, and Muthu's bankruptcy still remained freshly etched on his mind.

As he looked at his elderly parents, Teng knew he had to financially prepare himself for his retirement years.

Both Ma and Pa were already into their 60s — long retired.

Teng recalled when both his parents retired, they were lamenting about how they weren't used to not receiving any salary credited to their bank account, save for the monthly allowance given by Teng and his siblings. It took quite an adjustment for them to see their bank account balance dwindling each month as expenses were incurred with no commensurating income.

Both were in their silver years. They still had their savings in CPF and had withdrawn part of it when they turned 55. The withdrawn savings had been used for their holiday trip to China.

CPF

The CPF is a compulsory savings plan for working Singaporeans and permanent residents to fund their retirement, healthcare and housing needs. As an employment-based savings scheme, both employer and employee contribute a certain percentage to the fund.

In Teng's case, he did not enjoy this privilege. A taxi driver is by and large not considered as an employee of the taxi company but as an independent operator.

Upon reaching 55 years old, individuals can choose to withdraw part — 10 to 30 percent — of their CPF savings. Approximately one-third of retirees withdraw when they hit 55, with the average withdrawal amount being $11,000.

At 65, they begin to draw-down their savings in the form of monthly payments to help meet basic needs during their retirement years. There are various draw-down schemes to choose from depending on how much one needs each month and how much one wants to leave aside for dependents.

Monthly Income

Since turning 65, Ma and Pa started receiving their monthly CPF payments – $350 each – which would be credited into their POSB bank accounts. They were thankful for the monthly deposit as it helped defray household bills and provided some money for travel.

Although they did not receive an active monthly income, they were enjoying some passive income from renting out their Jurong flat. Peter had found four Malaysians working in Singapore who wanted to rent a flat near their workplace.

Ma and Pa's three-room flat was in its original condition – well-kept and with just bare necessities. They had left their living and dining room furniture behind for the tenants to use, along with some of the crockery. They couldn't bring these to Teng's house as there was already another set of furniture.

Given the poor economic outlook, they were lucky to have rented it out for $1,000 a month. But they needed to be prepared to reduce the rent should the economy deteriorate. If things worsened, they might have to go without a tenant for months. They could not assume that the rental income would be permanent.

But for now, the $1,000 rental income together with the $700 from their combined CPF drawn-down payments and the $500 from Teng were sufficient to cover monthly household expenses and the occasional vacation to a neighbouring country. They didn't want to depend too much on their children for their expenses.

Cards

Way before retirement, Pa and Ma already had a debit card each to help them with purchases without having to carry so much cash. It took them a while to get used to the notion of using a debit card. But they soon found the benefits of the plastic over cash.

Carrying cash could be troublesome. They could lose some in the midst of counting and keeping. "The new 50-cent coins look so much like the old 20-cent coins. I always have to look twice," thought Ma, as she adjusted her bifocal glasses.

Also, they might not have enough cash with them if they had forgotten to top up their wallet before going out. That had already occurred a few times, what with age making them quite forgetful. Or sometimes, they stumbled on an unexpected sales offer while shopping – only to find out that they didn't bring enough cash with them to make the purchase. A debit card was a convenient means to overcome these circumstances.

They also thought it convenient that they could use the debit card for purchases in many retail stores and supermarkets. Debit card purchases are quite widely accepted in Singapore. It also kept their wallet thinner for handy keeping in Pa's pocket or Ma's bag.

They had recently heard that there was now the Passion debit card offered by a local bank, which allowed senior citizens to enjoy a 5 percent discount on purchases at selected stores. "With things getting so expensive, it may be a debit card worth getting," Ma had thought. "A 5 percent discount is better than nothing."

Ma and Pa belonged to the generation well acquainted with financial hardship and were careful with how they spent.

Pa also had a credit card prior to retirement. Being a conservative man, with a debit card already in hand, he had thought that having one credit card on top of his debit card was more than sufficient. He had always been wary that having more credit cards might tempt him to spend more rather than have a tight grip on expenses.

But now with retirement, that credit card had become indispensable. Applications for new credit cards required income statements. But since most senior citizens have no income upon retirement, they are not eligible for new credit cards. Hence, that credit card that Pa had obtained before retirement would be the only that he could have, unless Teng appointed his father as his supplementary cardholder. Pa chose to hold on to his credit card just in case, but he still preferred to use his debit card.

Daily Routine

Every weekday morning, Pa and Ma would drop Ethan at the nursery-cum-kindergarten located at the next block. They would leave him there for the whole morning from Mondays to Fridays, and bring him home after lunch. It was good for Ethan to socialise with others beyond the family. It was there that he learned manners and how to overcome his shyness with strangers. It even taught him songs that Ethan would regale his grandparents with as they walked home.

"The wheels on the bus go round and round," Ethan sang and rolled his arms in circles, much to the delight of his proud grandparents.

With Ethan at the kindergarten, Ma and Pa would clean up the flat. Monday was a good day for house cleaning, since the wet market was closed that day. This gave them more time to do heavy duty cleaning.

For the rest of the week, they would do some simple cleaning up. While their clothes were in the washing machine, they would set off to the wet market together.

"Hello, Auntie," a young vegetable seller called out to Ma. The wet market was crowded with domestic helpers and retirees like Ma and

Pa, even though it was a weekday. "Today's *chye* (meaning 'vegetables') are very fresh. They've just arrived this morning. Come, slowly see."

"How much is the big *kailan* today?" asked Ma as she picked several stalks of the vegetable that she deemed fresh.

"Auntie, $3."

"You *siao* ah! You think I don't know how much they cost?" yelled Ma, pretending to be astonished at the price. She remembered not too long ago, she would have paid $2.50 for the big *kailan*. She understood inflation but still loved to bargain for a good deal.

"How about the baby *kailan*?" Ma asked hopefully as she wished to cook Teng's favourite vegetable for dinner. He had been working so hard as a taxi driver and needed all the nourishment he could get.

"$5 for this," said the vegetable seller as he grabbed a handful of the baby *kailan*.

"So expensive!" Ma remarked as she pulled a disapproving face.

"Auntie, I never cheat you. Things are getting more expensive," explained the young seller, somewhat afraid that the old lady would admonish him.

After all, the market stallholders saw Ma and Pa almost everyday. They wouldn't want to make a regular customer like Ma angry.

As retirees, Ma and Pa had plenty of time to spare. So why buy all the groceries at one go? Instead, they would buy just enough food for a simple lunch and a more sumptuous dinner for that day. Then they would return to the market the next day to buy food for that day's meals. This way, they could chat with the sellers and storekeepers every day, to while away some of the time they had until Ethan's class ended.

It was also easier on their back to carry a lesser load of groceries. Getting on in years, their walking was no longer as steady as it was before.

They were also mindful to wear non-slip shoes and watch their step while walking. They had attended a senior citizens' talk at the new community centre where a geriatric consultant advised them on several steps for graceful ageing, one of which was to wear anti-slip shoes to minimise falls.

Ma had told Pa, "That's just about the only thing we buy for ourselves. At our age, we have more than enough clothes. We don't need new clothes. Just wear the same old ones.

"Not like Siew Ling who buys clothes and shoes all the time. We're old already. Look so nice for what?" Ma said as she recalled how fast Siew Ling had spent the Growth Dividend Programme money that the government had given some years back.

"Except for Chinese New Year when we need new clothes to start a new year," reminded a conservative Pa who followed tradition. "And our occasional travel."

Ma would cook an all-in-one lunch meal for Pa and herself, as cooking multiple dishes for two could be challenging. How does one cook *ma po toufu* and roast chicken for two? Chinese dishes were best cooked in larger quantities for more people.

After lunch, they would saunter to Ethan's kindergarten and bring him to Nex to enjoy the air-conditioning in the shopping mall before heading home for his nap. Nex was where they would head to the supermarket to buy bread. The supermarket was also where Ma would look at fresh produce and meat and compare prices.

She often remarked, "So expensive. Why pay more for the packaging?" referring to the meat wrapped neatly on the polystyroam plate with cling-on wrapping. "Such wrapped meats are ok for working people because they find it more convenient to carry. And I think they also don't know how to choose. If you go to a wet market, it's smelly and noisy. And you must know how to choose which meat to buy. Young people nowadays don't know these things. They go for convenience."

Then they would return home for Ethan to take his afternoon nap while the grandparents watched the episode of the Korean drama, *Descendants of the Sun*, taped the night before.

Since moving in to the Serangoon flat, Siew Ling had interested them in watching Korean dramas. As time went on, Ma and Pa couldn't live without them. Ma would repeatedly compliment Song Joong-ki's good looks while affectionately calling him "Handsome Boy Boy", and Siew Ling would comment on Song Hye-kyo's clothes and fashion trends.

Community Centre Activities

Ma and Pa would also attend activities organised by the community centre. They had attended *qigong* classes, Chinese calligraphy lessons and even karaoke sessions.

"Today, Pa and I had such a good time. The karaoke songs were fantastic," Ma cackled while giving the thumbs-up. "They were oldies but goodies. There were songs from Teng Li-Chun. You know how much Pa loves Teresa Teng the Taiwanese singer. He was singing *Tian Mi Mi* so loudly even though he's so lousy at singing. So nostalgic!"

Teng had never seen his parents so happily occupied with activities before. Although Ma was reeling off the names of singers – Andy Williams, Dean Martin, Frank Sinatra – that were not familiar to him, it didn't matter. Most importantly, his parents were happy.

He thought that indeed, he and Siew Ling had made the right decision to move to Serangoon. The noise and higher electricity bills they had had to put up with when the community centre was under construction were worth it now that he could see his parents were enjoying themselves there.

One day, they noticed people were putting up red-and-white bunting outside the community centre.

"Must be for National Day," said Pa.

"Let's go and see," said Ma as they walked towards the community centre.

"'Golden Spending in Your Silver Years'. Nice title hor?" said Ma when she saw the poster pinned on the notice board at the community centre. There was going to be a talk organised by the community centre on retirement planning.

Although Ma and Pa had already retired for some years, they were still keen to attend. Maybe they could still learn a thing or two. Anyway, they had lots of free time on their hands.

Moreover, the talk would be held in the late morning – a perfect time for them as Ethan would still be at the nursery–kindergarten.

Retirement and Spending

Ma and Pa made sure it was an easy house cleaning chore on the day of the retirement talk. When they walked into the seminar room, they were surprised that there were already about 20 people seated, most of whom they recognised.

"Why are they here? They've retired long ago. This talk is for people who are about to retire, not retired," said a somewhat standoffish Ma.

"Aiyah! Look who's talking? They are like us. Lots of free time, so attend lor. If they don't attend, can you imagine how empty the room will be?" said Pa, keeping Ma in line.

The speaker was introduced as Ms Azlina, a banker. Her bank had undertaken some studies on how people spend before and after retirement and Ms Azlina expressed hope that the findings would prepare people ahead of retirement.

"As we progress through life, you find that what we buy and how much we spend on various items change at each stage of our life cycle.

"Do you remember the time when you spent a lot on clothes? When you see the latest fashion, you must also buy? When you see the latest handbag style, you must also have one?"

Some of the old folks nodded. The rest were quite reserved, or maybe, they just didn't understand what was going on. Or perhaps they were there because they had nothing else better to do.

"Now, how many of you would say you still spend just as much on clothes as you did when you were in your 30s or 40s?" asked Ms Azlina.

She could hear from the audience that they didn't buy as many clothes anymore.

"Too fat already. Cannot fit into those nice clothes anymore," joked a man loudly.

Everyone laughed. That was true. Their bodies weren't what they used to be.

"Ok. Now for the serious stuff," thought Ms Azlina.

[I]f we track the lifecycle consumption of an individual, it follows a 'hump' shape with expenditure peaking in middle age and then declining in the years that follow.

"Research demonstrates that if we track the lifecycle consumption of an individual, it follows a 'hump' shape with expenditure peaking in middle age and then declining in the years that follow."

Ms Azlina then drew a 'hump' shaped curve on the white board.

"This is generally how our expenses look as we get older. We spend the most in our 30s and 40s and spend

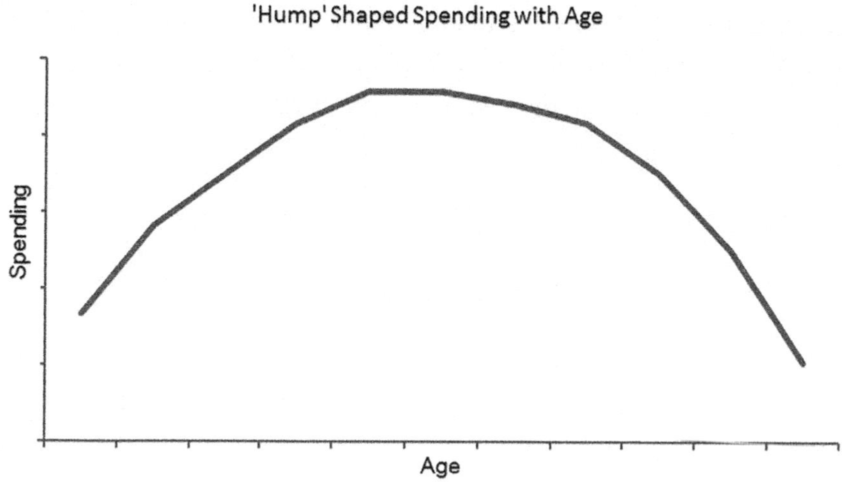

less as we continue to age. You can see we reduce our spending especially when we retire at around 60."

Ms Azlina continued.

"While it is not surprising that retirement curtails our expenditure, what we want to know is whether retirees cut down on all the things they buy. Are there things that are more likely to be cut down when one retires? Are there things that are less likely to be cut? Such information is important to know because it helps to understand how you as a retiree cope with your silver years — something critical in an ageing society like Singapore.

"So what my bank did was to use financial transactions of 180,000 bank customers to compare how Singaporeans spend across different age groups.

[O]nce you pass middle age, Singaporeans spend much less on apparel, small durables, dining and entertainment services than younger Singaporeans.

"We find that once you pass middle age, Singaporeans spend much less on apparel, small durables, dining and entertainment services than younger Singaporeans. Maybe the gentleman from the audience is right. We start to grow sideways and don't look good anymore even if the clothes were new. So why buy so many clothes?

"You can see this in the following charts on the screen.

Chart A. Total Card Spending

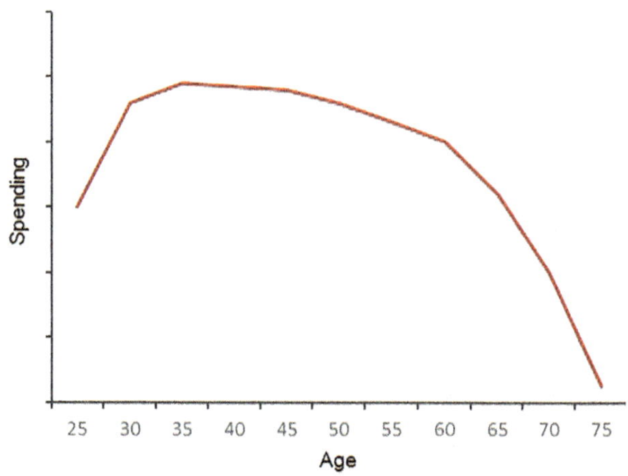

Chart B. Card Spending Expenditure Category

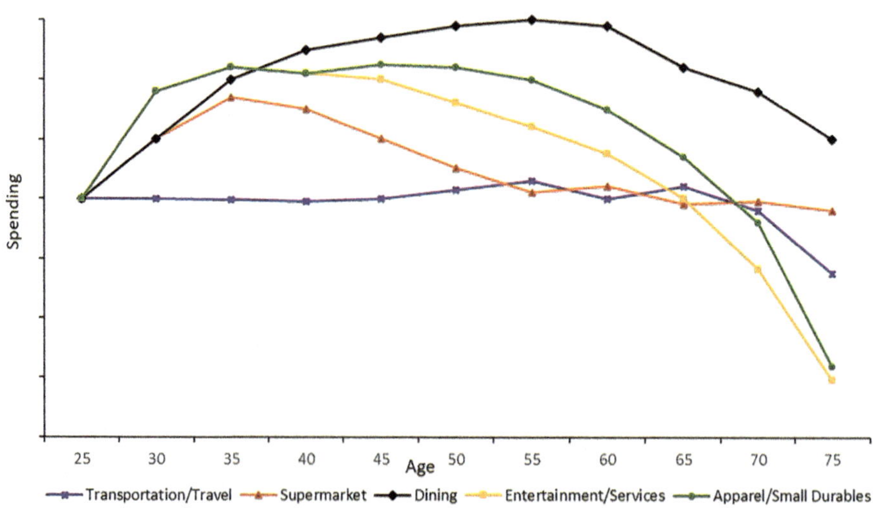

"Chart A shows the total spending using both credit and debit cards. You can see total spending on cards goes down when you retire at 60.

"But look at Chart B where you can see how much is spent on different items. Take 'Entertainment' for instance. We party less when we hit 45 years old. But we still want to wear nice clothes. So we still spend on clothes until we reach 60 years old, and then we spend less."

Ma turned to Pa and said, "That's just like us, isn't it? We don't buy so many new clothes anymore. Enough is enough."

"What about supermarket expenses?" asked Ms Azlina. "It's interesting that our supermarket shopping goes down the moment we are about 35 years old. Less dollar amount is spent at the supermarket.

[S]pending on debit and credit cards starts tapering when we are near retirement, and really tapers down after 60 years old.

"Overall, our spending on debit and credit cards starts tapering when we are near retirement, and really tapers down after 60 years old."

Use of Credit/Debit Card

"Now, how many of you have debit cards?" asked Ms Azlina.

Almost everyone raised their hands.

"Credit cards?"

About half raised their hands.

"So among those who have both debit and credit cards, which card do you use more often in your retirement years?" asked Ms Azlina.

The man who had joked about his expanding waistline volunteered, "I prefer to use debit card."

"Why might that be the case?" asked Ms Azlina.

"Well, I don't want to overspend since there's no more income coming in. With a credit card, I may forget how much I've spent. But with a debit card, because it deducts immediately from my bank account, I can see the balance and so I'm more aware of how much I've spent," replied the man.

Everyone nodded.

"Also, with a credit card, I have to write the cheque to pay the credit card bill. I don't know how to use electronic payment. At my age, I may forget to write the cheque. Then *kena* penalty for late payment," added the man.

"Thank you for your feedback. That was exactly what we found.

"We examined credit card and debit card spending separately for the different age groups. Look at Charts C and D. While monthly credit card spending followed the hump-shaped pattern that I showed you earlier, debit card spending is largely the same across Singaporeans under 50 years old. But those aged 50 to 70 spend more on their debit card than those under 50. You can see that in Chart D.

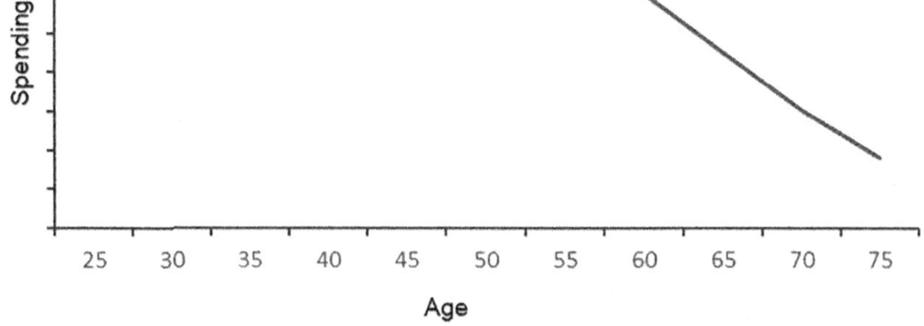

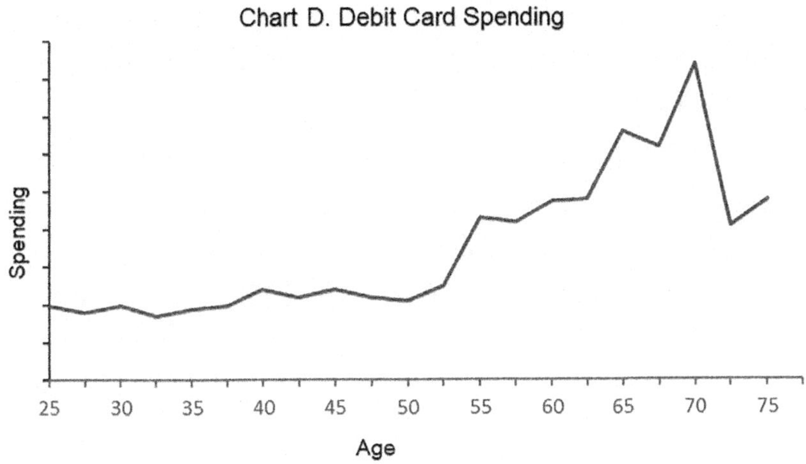

> **[O]lder Singaporeans are shifting their mode of payment from credit card spending in their earlier years to an increasing reliance on debit card spending in their later years.**

"So it looks like older Singaporeans are shifting their mode of payment from credit card spending in their earlier years to an increasing reliance on debit card spending in their later years."

Pa thought, "That's so like me."

"But, as a banker, my advice is this — If you are disciplined in your spending, then you should use your credit card instead of your debit card," advised Ms Azlina. "As its name says, a credit card gives you credit. That credit is about one month for you to pay for your expenses. So you buy something now but you don't have to pay for it until a month later. This frees up your cash for the time being for other purposes.

"However, if you pay by debit card, you are essentially paying by cash because it deducts from your bank account immediately. So if you are buying something very very expensive, it means that amount is not earning interest because it's gone from your bank account. But if you had paid using a credit card, that big amount would have earned one-month's interest. Of course, with interest so low these days, it isn't much. But still, the principle remains – interest that could have been earned is lost.

"Importantly, using a debit card means your cash is constrained. Remember what I had said earlier – if you had bought something using your credit card, the cash that you still have in hand is available in case an emergency pops up and you need to use it for that occasion. If you used a debit card, that cash is gone immediately.

"Of course, all these assume you are responsible in your spending and you pay your credit card bills on time. Late payment carries a very high penalty."

Post-Retirement Consumption

"Ok now. Let's move along," continued Ms Azlina.

"To see how retirement affects our consumption, we paired each retired individual in our sample with a similar non-retired individual based on observable characteristics such as age, race, gender, marital status, income, account balance and housing type. After which, we compared how the retirees and matched non-retired individuals differ on consumption.

On average, the retired Singaporean spends 12 percent less each month compared to the matched non-retired individual.

"On average, the retired Singaporean spends 12 percent less each month compared to the matched non-retired individual.

"But this varies considerably across product categories. The largest decline is in 'Transportation/ Travel', but other categories such as 'Supermarket', 'Dining', 'Entertainment/Services' remain fairly unchanged."

"Why do you think travel and transportation expenses go down?" asked Ms Azlina.

"Traveling is expensive. At our age, we have to go on package tours so that the tour guide can look after us. Each time we travel, it's easily more than $2,000 for a couple to go to a nearby country. That's a lot when you're not earning any income. So we travel less," offered Pa.

"It's so ironic. Last time, when we were young and earning, we had no time to travel because of work. Now we have the time but have no income," added someone from the audience.

"Yes, exactly. Which is why retirement planning is important. It ensures that retirees can still comfortably enjoy their silver years," reiterated Ms Azlina on the benefit of starting financial planning from a young age.

Food Expenditure

"However, we think that perhaps such card spending may mask reality as we did not consider cash being used in some of these purchases," Ms Azlina pointed out. "So, we used a second data set involving detailed data on consumer grocery spending. This data provided information on grocery spending, including shopping venue, the number of items purchased in each shopping trip, and product-level purchase details such as price and brand.

"I'm going to show you the charts on the *amount* spent on groceries and the *number* of grocery items bought.

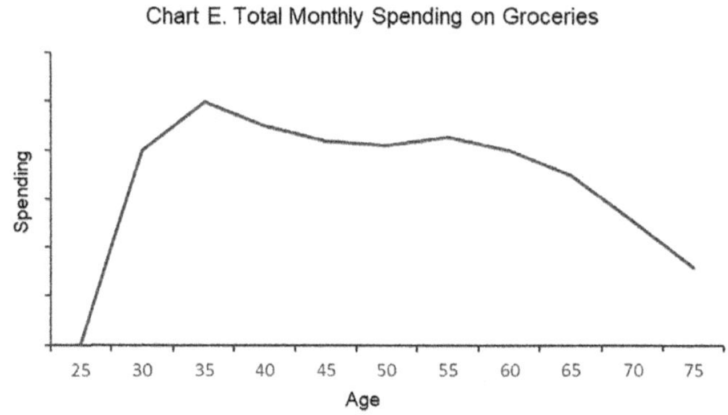

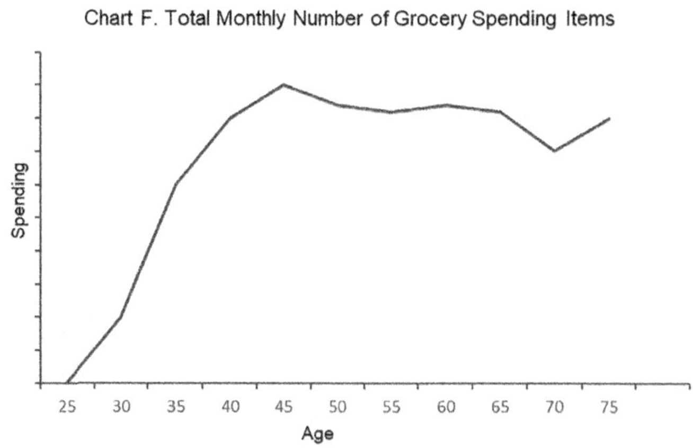

"On the top, Chart E, is the dollar amount spent on groceries. On the bottom, Chart F, is the number of grocery items bought.

"We found that home food purchase also exhibits the familiar hump-shaped pattern, i.e., the dollar amount spent on food declines as one approaches retirement. That is shown in Chart E.

"But look at Chart F. There is little evidence that older Singaporeans buy fewer items than younger Singaporeans. Regardless of whether they are working or retired, they buy the same number of food items. They have to eat, right?

"So we studied what types of grocery items they buy and where they buy them from.

[O]lder Singaporeans spend relatively more time shopping than younger Singaporeans. They will spend more on food items at the wet market and on store brand products.

"We found that older Singaporeans spend relatively more time shopping than younger Singaporeans. They will spend more on food items at the wet market and on store brand products.

Interestingly, their expenditure at high-end supermarkets was less than younger Singaporeans, suggesting that there is a substitution — as we retire and have more time but less disposable income, we substitute higher priced items with cheaper alternatives that require more time spent in purchasing."

Ma turned to Pa, "Hey, that's what we do. We go to the wet market every day and buy a bit at a time. We're so free."

Pa agreed and added, "And we don't buy so much from supermarkets now because the products sold there are more expensive than at the wet market."

Planning and Suggestions

Ms Azlina continued with providing advice to the participants on how to set aside their money to get better returns to last them through their silver years.

Before ending her talk, Ms Azlina asked the audience for suggestions on what could be done to help senior citizens. There were quite a number of suggestions.

Ma raised her hand and said, "My husband and I go to the *pasar* (meaning 'wet market') almost every morning to buy food and chit chat with friends. As there will be more and more senior citizens like us going to the *pasar*, I think it will help if the government can ensure that the *pasar* is clean and the floors not slippery. The lighting has to be brighter and maybe even railings can be installed so that it's safer to walk around."

Another person from the audience – probably a retired professional – volunteered, "We should have more store brand products as they are affordable, especially to retirees. Supermarkets such as NTUC are heading in the right direction with more house brands from toilet paper to cleaning detergents.

"I also think the present credit card rules may have to be relaxed given that older Singaporeans today are more educated and sophisticated than a generation ago. There are considerations of keeping retirees safe from robbery by carrying credit cards instead of cash. And especially for those who are more tech savvy, the current trend towards smartphone payments such as Apple Wallet may engender policy changes regarding credit card eligibility for senior citizens. I was in China a few months ago and was surprised that they use WeChat Pay and AliPay everywhere, even in their wet markets. You can just scan for your payments. That would help us too."

Ms Azlina noted down the suggestions for her bank to consider.

"That's a good point, especially now with online shopping increasing and brick-and-mortar shops experiencing a decline in sales revenue," replied Ms Azlina.

"The shopping centres and department stores are experiencing lacklustre sales because people find they can buy many other products online and sometimes, even at cheaper prices. To buy them online, you need a credit card.

"Can I ask how many of you have bought something online? Anything."

One man raised his hand. "I did. I piggy-back on my son's purchases on Amazon. I bought sports tape for my muscle aches. It's cheaper in

America than in Singapore. And over here, we have very limited options. Sometimes, I can't even find them when I need them.

"I wonder why it is cheaper in America than in Singapore for the same item. And these online stores can be quite aggressive. Sometimes, they offer free shipping if you buy a lot."

"Yes, online shopping offers you more variety – some items are not available in Singapore but you can buy them online. Sometimes, they are even way cheaper," Ms Azlina concurred with the participant.

"But you need to be careful of fraudulent practices. There are scams because there's money to be made and older folks are especially vulnerable," said Ms Azlina.

She waited for a while for more feedback.

Finally, the man who joked about growing waistline suggested, "Since senior citizens still buy the same number of food items as before, not working and earning a salary means they have to be careful with their grocery budgeting. For those in the lower income bracket, they are likely to be the hardest hit.

"Perhaps the government can consider providing some subsidies to help senior citizens with their retirement, particularly those in the lower income group."

Ms Azlina replied, "Well, I think the Silver Support Scheme is something that the government has done to alleviate the financial burden among retirees. I think some get quarterly cash subsidies of a few hundred dollars, right?

"While giving cash disbursements on a regular basis to the worst hit is one option, there are other alternatives to consider. For instance, maybe the GST can be waived on necessities that retirees buy or retirees may be given a card – similar to the senior citizen bus card

– that entitles them to a discount for selected items. We already have the Pioneer Generation card and CHAS (Community Health Assist Scheme) card for discounted medical and dental costs. The government can consider extending such discounts in the form of GST waivers for products that senior citizens buy."

As the talk ended, Ma told Pa, "Teng and Siew Ling should have attended the talk. Then they'll know not to buy so many clothes anymore." Ma was still concerned about how their children, including Teng, would manage after the passing of Pa and herself.

"Don't worry, he's a father now. He has grown. He'll manage," reassured Pa.

WANT TO KNOW MORE?

This chapter is based on Sumit Agarwal, Jessica Pan and Qian Wenlan, "The Composition Effect of Consumption around Retirement: Evidence from Singapore," *American Economic Review*, Vol. 105 (5), (May 2015), pp. 426–431; and Sumit Agarwal, Jessica Pan and Qian Wenlan, "Golden Spending in Their Silver Years," *The Straits Times*, (5 August 2016). http://www.straitstimes.com/opinion/golden-spending-in-the-silver-years

CHAPTER 20

Teng, Are You Grown Up?

It was National Day. The red-and-white Singapore flag, ironed crisp, hung smartly on the ledge of the balcony, fluttering amid the occasional warm breeze. The Town Council had strategically placed hooks along the balcony so that residents could hang the national flag to create a design for the block.

With almost all households co-operating with national pride, Teng's block was amassed in red and white, against the fresh cream coat of insulating paint.

Ethan had to wear a red T-shirt the day before as part of the nursery's celebration. Each child was given a small flag to cheer while watching the celebrations on TV.

Ma and Pa had said they were looking forward to watch the parade. It was a spectacle that they had never missed. They were eager to experience this proud moment with their grandson who was old enough to understand what's going on, making watching the parade together more meaningful.

Teng, however, had other ideas. He figured that since most people would be glued to their screens watching the National Day Parade, Universal Studios would probably be less crowded. The only crowd likely to be there were tourists or foreigners working in Singapore. He was still feeling sore from having to skip a visit to the theme park when the haze hit Singapore two years ago.

But Siew Ling would not hear any of it.

"How unpatriotic! How can you do this? What values are you teaching our son?" She gave him the evil eye.

"I'm just being stra-tee-gic. You know, being Singaporeans, we must learn how to survive since everybody is so *kiasu*," was Teng's response.

"And the answer is 'No'." Siew Ling's firm decision put an end to the conversation.

The Talk

After attending the retirement planning talk the month before, Ma and Pa had wanted to discuss with Teng about finances, especially since his CPF savings were limited — only his first job as a mechanic had contributed towards his CPF. Although Teng was far from retirement, it was never too early to start planning.

There was another matter that necessitated the urgency of discussing retirement planning with Teng. Ma had thought that perhaps the family would be bigger soon. Call it women's intuition but she thought Siew Ling had seemed to behave a little strangely of late, caressing her tummy every now and then, once too often. "Odd," she had thought, but had chosen to keep quiet in case she jinxed what could later be a happy announcement.

With National Day being a public holiday, Teng decided to take a break since there would be few people on the streets. Ma and Pa thought this would be an opportune time to discuss the matter with him.

"Eh, the other day, we attended the retirement planning talk. It was good. So informative," Pa started the conversation.

Ma and Pa knew that if Ma were to broach the topic first, Teng might think that there was a hidden agenda as had been the case with several past instances when Ma would sneakily weave in seemingly unrelated topics when she needed something from him.

Pa continued, "The lady, a bank officer, showed us how retirees spend on credit and debit cards, and their expenses on various types of products.

[B]ecause of no income coming in, retirees buy more from wet markets instead of supermarkets ... [T]he number of items they buy is still about the same but now, they spend less.

"Do you know, because of no income coming in, retirees buy more from wet markets instead of supermarkets? They still have to eat, shower, and shampoo. So the number of items they buy is still about the same but now, they spend less. How to spend less? They buy from wet market for meat and vegetables. Buy no-name brands for toilet paper, detergent and things like that. That's how retirees save money."

Ma was impatient to join in. She wanted to drum into Teng the need to save more, especially since she suspected another grandchild might be on the way. But she had to hold back or else Teng might just become defensive and not listen. It was agonising to keep quiet.

"It was quite an eye-opener," continued Pa. "We read all the time in the newspapers about planning for retirement. But it seems it still comes as quite an adjustment to many. They have to learn how to use their free time, otherwise their mind may rot. They must also learn to adapt in how they spend because there's no money coming in anymore. They just have to rely on savings and CPF."

Teng thought, "Is Pa hinting that he needs more allowance from me? Is he becoming like Ma? Wanting something from me by asking indirectly?"

"Teng, do you know much you have in your CPF?" asked Pa.

"Not much. Only from my first job as a mechanic," Teng replied.

"You know, I worked for 40-odd years," advised Pa. "Some of my CPF went to the HDB flat but I still have some leftover. The same for Ma too. Thankfully, we have that because it helps us with our retirement expenses. CPF now gives me and your Ma $350 each every month. And we get rental income from the Jurong flat, which we bought with our CPF savings. Otherwise, I wouldn't have been able to afford that flat. I'm so relieved we planned well and have the HDB flat for passive rental income.

"For you, you don't have CPF. So you'll need to be more careful and disciplined in your savings."

Ma couldn't take it anymore and jumped in, "Yah, Teng. You and Siew Ling must not anyhow spend money. Better to start saving now. $100 every month is also good. We can help you when we are still around. But next time, when we are not around, then how? Who's going to help you? And as the eldest in the family, you must be a good example to your younger brother and sister, on how to be a responsible family man."

Teng was moved by their concern. Ma and Pa had given much to help him. They had moved from their comfortable and familiar neighbourhood to live with them. At that old age, it took a lot to adjust to new surroundings.

Moreover, Teng had been the only child who needed his parents to help him take care of his son. His married sister did not need her parents' help. And his younger brother was living independently.

Moreover, as the eldest son, he felt a moral obligation to look after his parents.

And now, to hear them concerned for his finances, Teng was touched. He had grown to appreciate his parents' nagging. Even though he was now an adult and a father, his parents had much more to offer from their long years on Earth. They were a treasure trove of wisdom.

Über and Grab

Teng himself had similarly been somewhat anxious of late. Although his takings as a cab driver had not been too badly affected by the rising popularity of ride-hailing apps like Über and Grab, it was a phenomenon that he wasn't quite prepared for.

Über and Grab entered Singapore in 2013. For Über, Singapore was its first Asian foray. Grab, established in 2012 as MyTeksi in Malaysia, is a Southeast Asia focused app.

Many, including the young, are keen to be Über or Grab drivers, mostly as freelancers lured by the prospect of making easy money when their vehicle is idle or when they can offer a convenient ride-sharing service on their way to a similar destination.

About 20 to 30 percent of Grab drivers in Singapore are younger than 30 years old. The same profile goes for Über. Few however, rely on these companies as their primary source of income. They do not consider driving as a career. About half of Über's drivers clock less than 10 hours of driving a week. They are freelancers who provide point-to-point services for a variety of reasons such as funding for their higher studies or to support their families.

Competition for drivers is keen. Grab, for instance, offers enhanced perks for its taxi drivers with a monthly 8 percent Medisave contribution based on their earned incentives. Private-hire car drivers receive higher Medisave contribution rates at 10 to 15 per cent, depending on their performance.

[F]our years after Über and Grab entered the fray, there were almost 60,000 rental cars in Singapore — more than three times the rental car population prior to their entry. As many as half is attributable to private-hire services.

According to LTA statistics, four years after Über and Grab entered the fray, there were almost 60,000 rental cars in Singapore – more than three times the rental car population prior to their entry. As many as half is attributable to private-hire services.

In contrast, the taxi population dwindled. For the same period, the number of taxis downsized by 3 percent to an expected 26,500. While the dip may be minor, it is a contrast to the heyday when there was continuous growth.

Teng remembered reading in *The Straits Times*:

> "More cabbies are throwing in the towel and exiting the taxi trade, underscoring the stiff competition they are facing from private-hire services like Uber and Grab.
>
> Land Transport Authority data revealed that in the first 11 months of last year, the average rate of taxis that were unhired was 5.9 per cent, up from 4.2 per cent in 2015.
>
> More than 1,620 taxis are now sitting idle in the yards of taxi companies, up from 1,190. This, even as the total fleet of taxis in Singapore has shrunk, from 28,300 at the end of 2015 to 27,500 currently."

Reassurance

"Pa, Ma. I really appreciate how much you care for me. I understand the responsibilities ahead," said Teng to reassure his parents that he was mindful of his roles as son, husband and father.

"Don't worry. I have changed since having Ethan. I don't spend as much as I used to. I will continue to work hard. You know, despite Über and Grab, I'm still doing ok."

Ma and Pa looked at each other. They didn't know what Über or Grab were, but just kept quiet and let Teng continue.

Seeing the blank look on their faces, Teng realised that his parents were ignorant of these car-hailing apps. So he explained as best as he could.

"Über and Grab also offer something like taxi services. They are apps. Like WhatsApp is an app. You know the one where you can type a message and send to me?"

"Ah yes. I know WhatsApp," nodded his parents.

"Good. Über and Grab are also apps on your mobile phone but you use them to hire a private driver or one of the taxi drivers to pick you up and take you to your destination with a tap of a button on your mobile phone."

"Oh . . . So it's something like driver on-demand?" asked Ma.

"Yes, you could say that," nodded Teng.

"Über and Grab have made taxi driving more competitive. If Singaporeans want a taxi, they can choose from so many. If there's no taxi, there are private drivers available. And it's so easy with these apps. There's no need to call. And you can track where the driver is and how near he is to you."

"Aiyoh! Then you have less business?" Ma said with a worried frown.

"Yes and no. It's definitely more competitive – but Ma, I know where to pick up passengers. And I also signed up to be a Grab driver. So, my business has not been affected so badly," reassured Teng.

"Also, Singapore now allows surge pricing. Surge or dynamic pricing means the fare is not by meter but is adjusted depending on demand. When there's a lot of demand in one area, the fare automatically goes up. Über and Grab have surge pricing."

"Then why use Über or Grab? Might as well call for Comfort. Cheaper by meter, right?" shook Ma's head as she didn't understand why anyone would want to be held at ransom just because of high demand.

"Yah lor. I also don't understand. If I'm the passenger and I use Über, I will first check how much the price is. If it's too high, then I won't use, right? Instead, switch to Comfort or another taxi. Why get *ketuk*?" agreed Teng.

"That's why I think people don't like surge pricing. So in a way, there's still demand for my blue taxi," he explained.

"Oh another thing . . . The other day, one of my cab driver friend shared with me some figures about retirement. It was about taxi driver retirement.

[W]hen taxi drivers reach 55 years old, their fare takings drop by 3.5 percent. The number of hours driven also goes down.

"It showed that when taxi drivers reach 55 years old, their fare takings drop by 3.5 percent. The number of hours driven also goes down.

"I don't know whether it's because of age. But the moment we hit 55, everything just slows down.

"And you know what? This slowing down happens immediately after reaching 55. After that, the slowing down is less."

Ma, who was always the more chatty of the two, said, "I know why. They withdrew their CPF money!"

Pa jumped in, "Hmm . . . Maybe you're right. With the money, they can relax. So there's no need to drive as much as before. But where did they get the money from? I thought taxi drivers don't have CPF."

"Pa, not everyone is a taxi driver from Day 1. Most have worked elsewhere before. Maybe they switched jobs or they got retrenched. So the earlier jobs had contributed to their CPF, just like my mechanic job," explained Teng.

"Ah, yes. I supposed so. But your CPF is only a little bit from that job. So you must be very careful," reminded Pa.

"Don't worry, Pa. I know what to do," said Teng, attempting to reassure his parents again. "In fact, there's now a taxi company that employs drivers. That means drivers are paid a salary with CPF, like any regular job. And they don't have to pay for car rental or petrol. The taxis run on electric battery. And there's no shift too. They get to keep the taxi all the time. But of course, they have certain targets to achieve. If I think my taxi income is too low, I may switch to this other taxi company.

"Ma, Pa. You don't have to worry. I won't slow down. Not only will I work hard, I will also work smart. I will do my best as the man of the house," assured Teng.

The Parade

That year's National Day Parade was held at The Float@Marina Bay against the backdrop of the iconic Marina Bay Sands, Singapore Flyer and ArtScience Museum. As was always the case every year, tickets were hard to come by. The few who were lucky enough to be balloted would go to The Float hours earlier, bear the sweltering heat with sunglasses and hats and plenty of water and snacks, to ensure they get the best seats. Some would *chope* (meaning 'reserve') the seats with newspapers for family members who would join them later. Call it *kiasu*, but others would say they were patriotic.

In contrast, Teng and his family stayed comfortably at home. In the party mood, they had decked themselves out in red to watch the parade on TV.

His sister and her family were also there to join in the celebrations. As were Peter and his wife and kids. The children adored Ethan and loved playing with him.

"Peter, one day I must introduce you to my neighbour. I always say so but forget to do. He's a professor at NUS and he's interested in properties – not in buying properties but in studying property prices. I think you two can get along," Teng shared as he reminded himself to arrange for this get-together one day.

Just then, Siew Ling cried out loud, "Aiyah, look at the man – all so sweaty. Look at his perspiration. He must be smelly too!" as the cameraman panned across a section of the audience.

"This is so much more comfortable than under the hot sun. So sweaty. And what if it rains? Singapore's weather is so unpredictable," said Ma.

"For the atmosphere, Auntie. It's different at home and over there," said Peter.

The pre-parade started. The Singapore Armed Forces Red Lions parachute team gave a stunning free-fall display of skydiving, landing perfectly along the promenade right in front of the seating gallery, much to the applause of everyone both at The Float and at home.

"Daddy, next time when I grow up, I want to be like that parachute soldier," said Ethan as he pointed to the parachutist.

"Then you must work hard. You see – there are so many soldiers, right? But only a few can be part of the parachute team. So you must work hard, then you will be chosen to parachute," Teng coached his son.

"Daddy, how come you're not a soldier?" asked Ethan innocently.

"Because last time, daddy was naughty. Very playful. That's no good. Boy boy, you must study hard, OK? You need to study hard, then you can be on National Day Parade like that soldier and make mummy and daddy proud," said Teng in a warm fatherly tone.

As in previous years, the parade was engaging. There was an aerial salute by the Republic of Singapore Air Force's F-15SG fighter aircraft, a special tribute to 50 years of National Service.

The Singapore Navy gave an action-packed show involving naval divers jumping from a helicopter. Ethan was thrilled.

"Daddy, I want to be in the Navy. I can swim well," quipped Ethan.

There was a parade commander giving instructions to the military contingents in Malay. His voice had a presence – strong, hearty, and no-nonsense, it commanded attention. The camera had focused on him several times as he was the centre of attention until the performances began.

"Wow! Daddy, I want to be a parade commander," said an excited Ethan, having fast forgotten about the parachute soldier and naval diver.

"Huh? So fast change your mind?" laughed Teng. "No matter what, you must still study hard."

"I know what Ethan will be when he grows up," quipped Siew Ling.

Everyone looked at her.

"He'll be a big brother to his baby brother," Siew Ling smiled as she announced the good news.

"I knew it," said Ma to herself. Her instincts were still spot on.

"So now I must work doubly hard. Drive all night long," said a happy Teng. "And what will you call our second boy?"

"Ervin."

Just then, the parade ended with an arousing applause. And that was how Teng, his family and his friends decided that their lives would continue.

WANT TO KNOW MORE?

This chapter is based on Sumit Agarwal, Cheng Shih-Fen, Jussi Keppo and Koo Kang Mo, "Anticipated Income Shock and Labour Supply," (April 2017). Working Paper, National University of Singapore.

Other materials came from Christopher Tan, "Car Rental Numbers Surge Fueled by Private-Hire Players," *The Straits Times*, (12 September 2016); Christopher Tan, "Singapore Has Up to 1.5 Times More Private-Hire Cars Than Cabs," *Torque*, (25 May 2017); Belmont Lay, "Woman, 30, Reportedly Earns S$6,000 a Month Driving Grab for 9 Hours Daily in S'pore," *Mothership*, (13 March 2017); and Adrian Lim, "More Cabbies Leaving the Job Amid Stiff Competition," *The Straits Times*, (16 January 2017).

About the Authors

Sumit Agarwal, yoga fanatic and economics wiz, can untangle complex economics problems as adeptly as he can do most mind-boggling yoga poses including head stands. Who would have thought that this Visiting Professor of Finance from the National University of Singapore (NUS) Business School is as enthusiastic about financial economics as he is about fitness.

Previously, as the Vice-Dean of Research and the Low Tuck Kwong Professor at NUS Business School, Sumit had to take frequent taxi trips for his various meetings but he could never find a taxi when he needed one. That piqued his interest and the genesis of his research on Singapore.

Well known for his research relating to financial institutions, household finance, behavioural finance, and real estate and capital markets, Sumit brings a wealth of experience beyond intellectual rigour. He was a senior financial economist at the Federal Reserve Bank of Chicago and a senior vice president at the Bank of America.

With the ability to speak to the man on the street, Sumit is often quoted or featured in BBC, CNA, CNBC and Fox on issues relating to finance, banking, and real estate markets. His research is widely cited in leading newspapers and magazines like *The Wall Street Journal*, *The New York Times*, *The Economist* and *The Straits Times*. As he is passionate on sharing his knowledge, he also runs a blog on household financial decision making called Smart Finance.

Ang Swee Hoon lives and breathes marketing. As an Associate Professor of Marketing at NUS Business School, her students are often enthused by her passion in marketing. It comes as no surprise that Swee Hoon has been recognised on three consecutive occasions as an outstanding educator with the university's Teaching Excellence Award, putting her on the honour roll.

Her marketing mojo is evident in the leading textbooks *Marketing Management: An Asian Perspective* and *Principles of Marketing: An Asian Perspective* now in their 7th and 4th edition, respectively, that she co-authors with Philip Kotler, as well as in commentaries and media interviews. Swee Hoon also lends her expertise as advisor to several government boards.

Since obtaining her Ph.D. in Marketing from the University of British Columbia, Swee Hoon enjoys eclectic research including consumer happiness, counterfeiting, superstitions and advertising creativity. Her diverse research interests got her into reading on research outside marketing. This passion for acquiring new knowledge connected her with Sumit and Tien Foo, resulting in this book, *Kiasunomics©*.

Sing Tien Foo is the trivia king on all things related to Singapore real estate. Being a Dean's Chair Associate Professor and Deputy Head (Admin & Finance) at the NUS Department of Real Estate, and a Director at the Institute of Real Estate Studies, Tien Foo is likely to have no problem answering any questions on Singapore's property market. He serves in various capacities at government agencies including the Land Appeal Board, Ministry of Law, and the Council for Estate Agencies (CEA), Ministry of National Development.

His keen interest in real estate has seen him work on topics relating to options, real estate finance and securitisation, REITs, and housing price dynamics. One of the highs in Tien Foo's illustrious career is when his pet project on Singapore's NUS–REDAS real estate sentiment index received wide media coverage. He is a co-author of *Singapore's Real Estate: 50 Years of Transformation.*

An outstanding scholar with a Ph.D. from the University of Cambridge, Tien Foo's expertise in real estate goes beyond Singapore's shores. He lends his knowledge and expertise by serving on the board of the Asian Real Estate Society as its secretary, and on the board of the Global Chinese Real Estate Congress. He has also been invited as an expert witness in the review of land prices in Greater Taipei metropolitan area.

CPSIA information can be obtained
at www.ICGtesting.com
Printed in the USA
BVOW07*0748240118
506085BV00008B/1/P

9 789813 233362